D0931466

BUSINESS IN THE AGE OF INFORMATION

BUSINESS
IN THE AGE OF
INFORMATION
JOHN DIEBOLD

amacom

AMERICAN MANAGEMENT ASSOCIATION

Library of Congress Cataloging in Publication Data

Diebold, John, 1926-
  Business in the age of information.

  Includes index.
  1. Business—Data processing—Management.
2. Management information systems. 3. Commu-
nication in management. I. Title.
HF5548.2.D5113   1985   658.4'038   84-45782
ISBN 0-8144-5792-4

Printing number

10 9 8 7 6 5 4 3 2 1

**To
Billy**

FOREWORD

Henrik Ibsen wrote in 1882, "I hold that man is in the right who is most closely in league with the future." Although John Diebold would probably shun the title of futurist, he has been "in league with the future" for more than three decades. His record is enviable: In his 1952 book *Automation* he predicted the profound impact the computer would have on business and society—and he was writing two years *before* the first commercial installation of a computer! In the many years I have known him, John Diebold has consistently been a visionary, a thinker, a writer, and a controversial activist.

This augurs well for Diebold's latest collection of speeches and papers, *Business in the Age of Information*. In his first chapter, "Six Issues for the Future," he defines tomorrow's critical concerns as lucidly as if they were today's. As computer technology rapidly advances, it renders our current business concerns obsolete almost as quickly as we can cope with them. Issues such as competitive strategies, staffing, organization, accounting conventions, and technological change all raise troubling questions for those who manage information systems and for nontechnical managers alike.

In the next two chapters—"National Information Policy and Economic Consequences" and "International Business in the Information Age"—Diebold challenges us to consider the international community in which businesses operate. No corporation works in a vacuum. National policies relating to information technology in the areas of international trade, privacy, copyright, antitrust regulation, and other areas will have profound repercussions for businesses of all kinds. Because of technology's many, often subtle interplays with business and society, the most important economic and technological developments may come from unanticipated areas. Diebold widens the perceived domain of the business executive.

In another chapter, "Seventeen Possible Future States," Diebold takes another candid look into the future. Will electronic data bases supplant traditional print newspapers? Will the home computer become as ubiquitous as the telephone? What will this mean in terms of business opportunities? The author asks us to expand our view of the future, thereby creating a new context for the way we view technology *today*.

His final chapter, "Information Technology: Unleashing a New Era of Competition," explores six ways in which the computer is fundamentally changing the ways businesses compete, from new products and services to new business relationships—and even new ways of defining the mission of the enterprise. As always, Diebold has one eye on the future: natural language voice systems, artificial intelligence, household robots, and even computer implants in human bodies have a role to play in the competitive strategies we forge today.

Business in the Age of Information is certain to be a vital tool in helping today's business leaders confront the staggering challenges that the technological revolution has thrust upon us—and, we hope, enabling them to turn those challenges into opportunities.

Dean Russell Palmer
The Wharton School

CONTENTS

Chapter 1

SIX ISSUES FOR THE FUTURE

The changes wrought by computers are creating parallel upheavals in business and society. Technology is changing not only the tools we use, but our traditional assumptions regarding human resources, staffing, organization, competitive strategies, accounting conventions, and the role of business in society. Managers can no longer rely on the "business as usual" approach. The corporations that lead the way will be those that capitalize on change, forging policies with an eye to the issues of the future.

This chapter is adapted from a speech presented to the 61st plenary meeting of the Diebold Research Program on the occasion of its 20th anniversary, October 18, 1983, in Grenelefe, Florida.

1

In October 1963, at the first meeting of the Diebold Research Program, we put forward a construct of what we thought the next generation of computer would look like. At the time our construct was greeted with total disbelief. Yet it described perfectly the IBM 360—a landmark system in the history of computing—which was announced in the spring of the following year. That winter, the vice president for engineering of one of the large computer companies and his superior, the executive vice president, explained to me in detail why, for engineering reasons, for economic reasons, for a whole range of reasons, the system we had envisioned could not exist. That was 60 days before the 360 was announced.

During the first 20 years of its history, the Diebold Research Program has championed numerous positions that were extremely unpopular for long periods of time. Distributed data processing was one of those; the Program's initial reports on the subject were almost universally rejected. The same was true of data base management systems, the importance of real-time systems, and a number of other new concepts we put forth. We also predicted in our early meetings not only that the computer would become a very important capital good, but that it would gradually also become a consumer product. Clearly that is happening today, with the revolution in home computers.

The point of these examples is to demonstrate how far we've come in 20 years, and to provide a context for looking ahead. I have identified six issues for the future that pose serious questions for computer professionals and business professionals alike. Some of what I suggest, especially with respect to future technologies, may be greeted with the same kind of skepticism and disbelief that my colleagues and I have experienced in the past. And yet, with the clarity of hindsight, these same ideas may one day be widely greeted with a shrug of acceptance, as if to say, "Of course, it's obvious—that's the way it's done."

1. ORGANIZATIONAL ISSUES

The following five organizational areas and issues—the human interrelationships and hierarchies—associated with computers and communications will have a decided impact on the shape of the computer professional's job.

1. *Management information systems (MIS).* Generally this area is highly organized and well developed; reports to someone at the officer level in large companies.
2. *Office automation.* Typically it reports to someone at a lower level than MIS does, but there are many different organizational models. It is often a clerical activity that is not part of the computer systems department. (All too often the motivation behind automating the office today has been clerical savings, when the real focus ought to be on improving the productivity of managers and professionals.)
3. *Communication systems.* This function reports to people at different levels in different organizations, although more and more report to the MIS directors. Communication systems have generally been organized in a helter-skelter way at fairly low levels in

organizations. Until now, they had tended to focus on one source of supply: AT&T. But suddenly we have what my colleagues have been describing as "option shock": a vast number of alternatives available in voice and data communications. The problems in network analysis, for any large company, generally far exceed the capability of the individuals responsible for handling this function.

4. *Manufacturing systems*. These include computer-aided design and computer-aided manufacturing (CAD/CAM) as well as increasingly complex factory systems integrated with corporate information systems. As the investment level picks up in the U.S. economy, the developments in the manufacturing area will become a very intense and very interesting part of the total picture.

5. *End users (nontechnical professionals)*. In many organizations, computing is beginning to become a user-driven activity and a user-driven development, with all kinds of implications for the MIS director. It means that the MIS professional goes from being a wholesaler to a retailer, something that has not been done in most organizations without the most fundamental soul searching. It means that troubling new policy questions arise as the end user becomes a very important driving force in computing through the expanding use of microcomputers.

Traditionally, these five areas have developed separately in many organizations. Integrating the functions into a holistic systems approach is a prerequisite to comprehensive information resource management (IRM), in which information is disseminated to those who will use it in their decision-making and professional capacities.

The integration process is extremely complex, time consuming, and expensive. The principal barriers, however, are not technical but human factors. We have a very poor understanding of information flow, human interrelationships, and the structure of work in the corporation. Yet the human organization has everything to do with how we organize information in our electronic systems. Bringing the five organizational elements into line within the context of an over-arching information systems strategy becomes crucial in light of the emergence of information technology as a *key determinant of competitiveness* within more and more industries.

How does the computer affect the competitiveness of industries? One example is the incorporation of computer capability into more and more products, such as credit cards with computer chips, automobiles with "trip computers" that can tell a driver when to turn, or dishwashers whose sales appeal depends upon having microprocessors built into them. The computer capability lets the manufacturer differentiate its products from the competition's.

More than a decade ago, the chairman of one of the major German companies came to my firm and said, "Help us get into the microprocessor business, into the chip business." When I asked, "Is this for diversification?" he said, "No. Our customer, Daimler, in order to sell Mercedes-Benz in the future, must provide a sophisticated information system within the Mercedes. That's going to determine the competitiveness of the Mercedes in the world market." At the time it was a far-sighted, intelligent comment, and his company began to make some very serious moves in that direction.

The impact of computers is being felt not only in products, but also in distribution systems: a manufacturer can jump over layers of middlemen and tailor its products to meet its buyers' needs. A bank can deliver electronic services via automated teller machines, or directly to the home computer, so that old criteria of competitiveness such as the number and location of bank branches are no longer relevant.

In publishing, too, we have the capability for transmitting information electronically, rather than via paper manuscripts. I'm on the board of directors of Prentice-Hall, and I was astonished to learn at a recent meeting that it planned to publish, in a three-month period, almost 300 books on computers, many with floppy disks as part of the book. One of its bread-and-butter products, a looseleaf tax service, has been completely converted into on-line services. Clearly, information technology is a very serious determinant of competitiveness when a major publisher finds its products taking a great many new forms.

Other publishers offer magazines on floppy disks; for example, a children's magazine contains "interactive" stories in which the child can choose how the story ends. We're just at the earliest stage of this, but it is clear that many more industries are going to be vastly different from the way we know them today. The patterns of competition are being changed by computer technology.

In light of the five organizational elements I have described, and the recent emergence of information technology as a strategic force in the corporation, what shape will the MIS professional's job take? What ought it be for the best interest of the enterprise? Will it become more concerned with higher level strategic questions, such as how to deploy information technology as a competitive weapon? Will office automation, telecommunications, manufacturing systems, and end-user computing become centralized under the MIS umbrella? All these are important questions. From a personal standpoint, the MIS director has a great many more career options now than he or she had a couple of years ago.

2. HUMAN DEVELOPMENT

As information technology becomes increasingly recognized as a determinant of competitive effectiveness in businesses, the profiles of the type of people we need to develop in the MIS area changes.

A whole array of staffing and human development questions arise. The ideal candidate for the MIS job is not the technician but the entrepreneur: a person who is interested in what the company's product is, whether it's an insurance company, a manufacturing company, or whatever. The need for a businessperson's understanding of information technology as a business resource raises a wholly different set of job requirements.

It's a big problem, and we know it because more and more CEOs are asking my firm what to do about it. They say, "We have a super MIS activity, but how does it fit in with our future goals? We know that computer technology is changing the way businesses compete, changing payment systems and products and distribution channels. Where do we get the human talent that can help us forge strategies in this area? Who is going to have the imagination to do a first-class job—not on yesterday's method of doing business, but on how we should be doing business tomorrow?"

These questions present an "open sesame" to the entrepreneurially minded MIS professional. Even if he or she is not so inclined, the MIS manager is still the logical one whom senior management will seek out to help in this area. What kind of people should the MIS manager develop as successors? And what other possible human interfaces, from other departments, might help bridge the gap between corporate management and MIS?

3. ACCOUNTING CONVENTIONS

A third issue to examine in the future is the problem of accounting conventions that are used with respect to information systems. They affect the way our economy moves, the way individual companies operate, and what MIS accomplishes.

For example, the terms of reference that are used in chargeback systems determine an internal market, and thus determine what kind of software products and systems will be developed. What do you capitalize, what don't you capitalize? This question becomes very important for systems that cost hundreds of millions of dollars to develop. The conventional procedure is to expense everything, but we are beginning to get into situations in which the scale of the system is so great that very few businesses can afford to do that.

One of the accounting issues we raised some 20 years ago, in one of the first meetings of the Diebold Research Program, has yet to be resolved: we still don't have a measure for the *time value of information*. Most of our system purchase decisions are made on the basis of displaced costs: of equipment, of people. Very few of the decisions are made on the basis of the time value of the information; that is, the value of increased effectiveness, better decision making, and more time freed up for management. Instead, we cross our fingers and say, "Well, we think we need this system and therefore we're going to pay for it." If we could make a few serious moves toward understanding the time value of information, it would be helpful in determining where to go. That's an issue we would all like to avoid, but it's an important issue.

The failure to measure the time value of information also relates to the great analytical void that exists in the area of methodology. It is most pronounced in office automation, where very few solid analyses have been conducted regarding the role of information in an organization, the nature of human interfaces, how the internal interventions are made, and the very delicate and constantly changing balance between machines and people. Serious gaps exist with respect to methodology, and we are not allocating resources to close those gaps.

4. AGENT OF HUMAN CHANGE

As is true of all the major technological breakthroughs in history, information technology represents an agent of human change. Very early in my firm's history—more than 20 years ago—we identified three stages of human change: First, computers are used to do the same job in a different way. Second, the job itself changes. Third, the greatest change of all occurs in society. And this opens to the enterprise the greatest opportunities of all.

Examples of the third stage are now starting to appear. At one extreme, you have "hackers" like the infamous "414s" in Milwaukee, who used computers to break into various networks. Although the 414s may have done damage and may indeed have committed crimes, they did perform a service for all of us, because they shook everyone up and brought some serious security issues to the forefront.

At the other extreme, we find examples of positive social change in the emergence of "electronic cottages." Small computers make it possible for individuals to work in the comfort of their homes, avoiding commuting costs and all the distractions of the corporate office. Such flexible work arrangements open new opportunities for businesses, which now have far greater options in whom they hire and where those workers are located.

Clearly, we are experiencing an extraordinary phenomenon in that society's patterns are changing as a result of the technology. That creates opportunities for business as well as problems. Business history has shown us that great opportunities occur when there are changes in society. Most businesses that try to go on just as they had before will fail. As it becomes more expensive and more difficult to do things the old way, a small number realizes that the rules of the game have been changed and see great opportunities in this change—those become the great growth businesses. The human element is the key to whether you achieve productivity from the technology. Surprisingly little original research work is done on this. One group, the Public Agenda Foundation, is doing a serious project on productivity and the human factors in introducing advanced technologies. This aspect of technology is extremely important.

5. TECHNOLOGY IN THE FUTURE

The ability to look ahead has always been the driving force and the strength of the information technology field. Some of the techno-economic changes that are coming up have considerable significance. I think the problem is that we hear about them too early on, and then they seem to take a long time to develop. We thus tend to discount them, and then suddenly they're upon us and making a big impact.

For example, each year we at our firm try to spend a day at Bell Laboratories, a day at the IBM Systems Research Labs, and time at other labs. I recently noticed changes in the notes I take in these sessions. There are always new acronyms, and I'm always appalled by them—BIPS for billions of instructions per second, for example. Suddenly I found that I was starting to have notes about inverse transformational structures, semantic interpretation rules, string transformations, and all sorts of other strange things. The group of Ph.D.'s who had been briefing us were linguists, and they were trying to solve the language problems encountered in voice response systems. The cost of processing will no longer be prohibitive by the time they get the language problem solved, and this is very serious research. The role of spoken language and man-machine dialog is something we've all discounted because we all know the problems in it. For example, when the machine tries to translate "out of sight, out of mind," it comes out "blind and crazy." This is just one of a series of very funny problems in translation. We all know the difficulties, but the fact is that systems will not always be as limited. In a few years, natural language voice systems will become a tremendously important development.

There are two other areas that very few people are focusing on which I'd like to look at, because I think that 20 years from now, when we look back on this phase, they will be the big news items: neurobiology and biogenetics. Basic research in these fields is being conducted at Rockefeller University and the Carnegie Institution. Biogenetics bears great similarities to the computer field and I believe that the two fields are going to converge.

We talk about reaching the limits of storage capacity after the next two generations of chips. But chemically the "storage" capabilities within each cell of our bodies is far beyond that of any chip. Each cell has a ribbon of DNA two meters long. In that strand of DNA, which is one-ten-thousandth of an inch in diameter, there are 3 billion bits of information. (That may or may not be the limit of information storage capabilities.) So when we talk about limits in terms of a silicon wafer, we're talking about a very early phase in understanding what density of storage is possible. If you could enlarge the width of a DNA molecule to that of computer tape, the proportional length would be the equivalent of once around the earth—we've got that in each cell. Each DNA molecule carries 10 million genes, of which 1 percent are active. Nobody knows about the other 99 percent. Some Nobel laureates think these are genetic garbage, and some Nobel laureates think Nature doesn't work that way and that we simply don't know enough yet to understand what the rest of it is.

Of those 10 million genes, we have 100,000 different working entities that we're aware of, each of which has a different protein. Of those, 1,000—1 percent—have names and have at least been identified. More tangible evidence exists about 100. And so far, despite all the discoveries in this field, 10 have actual medical uses. So we are not even at the dawn of understanding in that field.

When people in the field of biogenetics talk about copiers and tape readers, they don't mean Xerox 914s— they mean RNA. RNA is a tape reader and a copier. Enzymes are readers. A few new companies in the United States today are actually working on developing organic computers. The chemical processes are very slow, but we are beginning to see serious work on molecular structures for computers.

Every computer we have today is a von Neumann computer, based on design principles put forth by John von Neumann. Today, some noted neurobiologists think that the human body holds the key to totally new forms for computers—perhaps the first non-von Neumann machine. Gerald Edelman, who won a Nobel Prize for biogenetics, has made two discoveries in the field of neurobiology that he believes are much more important than the one for which he got his Nobel: discoveries in the bases of memory structure and of logical design machines that totally depart from a von Neumann machine. There is a great difference of opinion among distinguished scientists in this area, yet I cannot help but think we are going to find dramatic changes in the computer field as a result of work in neurobiology.

I've often cited a cartoon which, after 30 years, still stands up very well, and that is a Charles Addams cartoon from *The New Yorker* in which two caterpillars are talking to one another. Above them a moth emerges from a cocoon, and for the first time unfurls its lovely wings. One caterpillar says to the other caterpillar, "You'll never get *me* up in one of those things." That's held up for the last 30 years, and as far as I can see it still applies today. The areas of technology that are really going to affect all of us in the coming decades are viewed by everybody the same way: "You'll never get me up in those things." But the changes are nonetheless inevitable.

6. DETERMINANT OF INTERNATIONAL COMPETITIVENESS

The last of the six key issues we face involves information technology as a key determinant of international economic competitiveness. Japan's Ministry of International Trade and Industry (MITI) does not assign a yearly quota to information technology (as it does to other industries) because, according to their printed "vision of the 1980s," information technology is so fundamental to Japanese competitiveness in every other industry category that it simply is a category by itself. It's not a question of how many computers are sold, or word processors, or terminals, or anything else; it's a question of how the economy depends on, and will be determined by, this field.

French President Francois Mitterand has taken exactly the same kind of position. And the Minister of Technology of another Western European country came to see me to discuss the same kinds of questions: What can that country do to maintain economic competitiveness for the remainder of this century? What should its national policies be regarding information technology?

The United States is, for now, the leader in high technology. We're ahead for a variety of reasons. We have a highly mobile and well-educated population. In addition, people can fail here without stigma—a person can leave a large company, fail as an entrepreneur, and go back to work for another large company, or start again. That is not true in Japan, where one would "lose face" under these circumstances, and it's not true in Germany, where bankruptcy laws impose 28 years of liability and thus discourage risk-taking. We have a number of cultural characteristics that help foster innovation. The question is, how do we maintain those characteristics?

We're aware of the problem of innovation among the Soviets. I learned at a meeting in Ottawa recently of a fascinating case in which a small Silicon Valley bank was bought by a Singapore company that turned out to be a Russian-controlled company. The bank was bought specifically to provide funds for failing Silicon Valley companies in order to gain a position in the backing of these companies, and therefore to get some leverage to acquire technology. It's a documented case that indicates just how important technological innovation is to the Soviets. I'm even more interested in how it is viewed by other industrialized countries. We in the States tend to evade the problem of developing coherent national policies regarding information technology. Most other countries are focusing very hard on it.

These, in sum, are the six issues I would choose as being ones that ought to be studied hard now and in the decades just ahead of us. Some are more pressing than others, but those that aren't as pressing—for example, some of the intellectual problems of methodology and accounting conventions—may turn out to be more important in the long run.

I'd like to end with a comment from the *Dialogues of Alfred North Whitehead,* the British philosopher and a favorite author of mine:

> It is the business of the future to be dangerous, and it is among the merits of science that it equips the future for its duties. . . . In the immediate future there will be less security than in the immediate past, less stability. It must be admitted that there is a degree of instability which is inconsistent with civilization, but on the whole, the great ages have been the unstable ages.

Chapter 2

NATIONAL INFORMATION POLICY AND ECONOMIC CONSEQUENCES

The information technology industries influence virtually every other industry sector, both nationally and internationally. The complexity of the technology and the economic importance of its many interactions with business and society make effective policy formation exceptionally difficult on national, let alone international, levels—and policy generally lags well behind advances in technology. National policies with respect to this dynamic cluster of industries will have sweeping economic consequences for businesses everywhere.

This chapter is based on a paper delivered to the Institute for International Economics in Washington, D.C., on June 25, 1982.

Information technology is a large and rapidly growing high-technology industry with direct impact on office as well as factory productivity. Moreover, information technology is unique in its pervasiveness, for it is incorporated in, and is changing the competitive basis of, a wide range of industries—from auto and consumer appliances to heavy machinery. It is having a dramatic impact on services such as banking and publishing.

What do we mean by *the information technology industries?* This sector is, in fact, a cluster of industries whose products and services provide for the original entry of information and its subsequent processing or treatment, indexing, description and clasification, storage and retrieval, as well as its transport and communication.

■ The services component includes communications, data processing bureaus, information or data base providers, financial services, electronic publishing, and programming services.

■ The manufacturing component includes computer equipment, communications equipment, office equipment, and semiconductor devices. In the manufacturing sector, the cost of computer performance has been declining at a rate of 20 percent or more per year.

In addition to being a prime example of a "sunrise" industry (at a time when so much of the industrial policy literature is addressing the problems of "sunset" industries), the dynamics of the information technology industry poses a variety of international economic problems:

- The disparity between the rapid rate of technological change and the nature of its swift impact on other industries, on the one hand, and the much slower rate of change of pertinent public policies, both nationally and internationally, on the other.
- The difficulty each nation faces in determining what is in its national interest vis-à-vis information technology, and how to achieve these interests domestically, as well as what it should and can do about the international aspects of these problems.
- The complexity of technological development and the economic importance of its many interplays with virtually all other aspects of society makes the development of effective policy coordinating mechanisms exceptionally difficult on both national and international levels.
- Because of its impact on international competitiveness of virtually all other national industries, the policies which a less developed country (LDC) pursues to ensure a domestically viable information equipment industry can have particularly negative effects.

National industrial policies regarding this key industry vary widely. In the United States the basically laissez faire approach has been overlaid with a complex vestige of old regulations and attitudes that can put at risk the country's leading position in this evolving industry. The situation is the result of the disparity between the rapid pace of scientific/technological development and the slow pace of the U.S. public policy process, and the convergence of the brand-new computer industry with the established and highly regulated communications industry. In stark contrast, several other industralized countries have recognized the seminal importance of information technology. However, most have shown little ability to translate their vision and considerable technological brilliance into a strong economic position, although Japan is a notable exception.

The international economic issues raised by the information industries are of considerable interest for they can provide examples of the policy problems of sunrise versus sunset industries:

- A harsh but not inaccurate caricature of the current U.S. view has it that Nippon Telephone and Telegraph Co. offers to buy telephone poles from the United States in return for a license from AT&T that assists Japanese suppliers in selling advanced electronic equipment in the United States.

- Japanese regulations prevented the importation to Japan of American-made integrated units containing more than 200 circuits per chip (circa 1974) until a date that coincided with the Japanese semiconductor manufacturers' development of the capability of producing competitive products.

- To be fair, AT&T in 1981 chose Western Electric over a lower bid by Fujitsu for a major fiber optics telephone trunking system in what had been advertised as a completely open competitive procurement.

In other words, the information technology industry provides almost daily examples of international economic problems. The question for today is whether these problems are new or unique and therefore whether they require particular attention or policy mechanisms.

Our choice of the information industry as the focus of trade policy considerations is consistent with the recent MITI statement in Japan that information technology is probably the key determinant of international economic competitiveness during the remaining years of this century. National success in dealing with this new industry requires coherent national industrial policies, as well as successful resolution of the relevant international economic issues.

IMPACT OF THE INFORMATION TECHNOLOGY INDUSTRIES

The information industries include the following:

1. The semiconductor industry, including companies that manufacture components, subsystems, and test equipment.
2. The computer and peripheral equipment and systems industry.
3. The telecommunications equipment and systems industry.
4. The office equipment and systems industry.
5. Information processing services.
6. Telecommunications services.
7. Electronic publishing services.
8. Programming services for computers and electronic systems.

Primary Benefits

In their primary role, the information industries represent, in their own right, a major direct contribution to the U.S. economy. The value of domestic U.S. shipments or revenues by these industries amounted to approximately $171 billion in 1981. In other countries the contribution of information is generally proportionately smaller.

In addition to the actual revenues, the export component of these revenues must be considered. It is substantial and amounted to approximately $17 billion in 1981 for the United States. If we exclude the service components, that represents 20 percent of the value of U.S. domestic equipment shipments. The $8.8 billion positive balance of trade of the information industries represented a very strong contribution to the U.S. economy in 1981.

The already pervasive diffusion of information technology into every home is indicated by the growth in installed "active element groups" (AEGs). An active element group is that electronic technology necessary for one bit of logic or one bit of memory. Eight bits are required to identify or store one alphanumeric character. The average home in the United States utilized 700 active element groups in 1970 and 7,000 in 1980. The pace will increase in the 1980s and the average U.S. residence is predicted to have several hundred thousand AEGs in by 1990, suggesting that every home in the United States will be a consumer of the electronic information industry. This follows the trends of other industries where initial applications are industrial, but products and services eventually become pervasive throughout society.

The sustained growth of the information industries is predicated on the continued increase in functional capability of semiconductor chips and on the declining cost per function. Increasingly efficient information technology will have a more indirect impact on international competitiveness as the incorporation of more powerful miniature computers into consumer and industrial products—from autos and sewing machines to video games—will determine the salability of these products on world markets.

Secondary Effects

In addition to the large direct economic contribution, important secondary and tertiary benefits arise from the development and application of information industries. The secondary effects from information technology include:

1. The development of entirely new industries.
2. Improved operations of existing industries.
3. The development of new and expanded services.

Secondary benefits underline the importance of the information industries, for the advancement of computer and communications technologies must necessarily precede their inclusion in industrial equipment and processes and consumer goods. Secondary effects of the information industries are pervasive and very important. Unfortunately, we are not aware of any studies that quantify the secondary effects of the information industries on national economies and they are treated anecdotedly. Marc V. Porat, in a study entitled *The Information Economy* (Stanford University Institute for Communication Research, Report no. 27, vol. 1, August 1976, p. 189) has attempted to indicate the growth of employment in the information industries in the United States and has suggested that half of the work force is engaged in information-intensive tasks.

Among the several information technology examples that broadly affect the public, note first the growth of international communications, in which satellites are used to permit live video transmission and to improve the quality and lower the cost of voice and data communications. Substantial benefits accrue to the economy and to society from better and cheaper communications. Another example with international implications is the development of worldwide computerized airline reservation systems that can provide instantaneous confirmations. A third example is the availability of remote automated teller machines that permit individual banking and other transactions after regular business hours.

Among industrial users the process industries, such as steel, chemicals, and petroleum, have been improved by feedback control systems incorporating electronic instruments and microcomputers. Now it is the discrete manufacturing industries' turn to incorporate microcomputer-based robots and controls to improve quality and reduce costs.

Among consumer goods, "smart" appliances, automobiles with digitized voice-alerting functions, calculators, digital watches, and Pac-Man® video games are all manifestations of the incorporation of electronics into everyday products.

Concern that information technology in its "automation phase" can displace workers rather than create employment is most often articulated in those European countries with a strong labor participation in government. There are and will be dislocations in certain industries as well as opportunities in others with the possibility of local labor force stresses. However, the failure to apply advances in information technology leads to noncompetitiveness and/or dependency on government subsidies.

The list of secondary impacts could be greatly expanded, but the important point is that *the information industries are central to the economic development and important to the personal development of our society.* Successful application of information industry products and services to other industries provides the basis for improved competitiveness of those industries. Improved competitiveness of existing industries and development of new industries are the most important secondary effects.

Tertiary Effects

Tertiary effects arising from the information industry developments have and will continue to have worldwide consequences. These include improved and expanded computer literacy, which will enable large numbers of people to directly access and participate in the information processing revolution. In addition, the increased availability and lower cost of communication will stimulate individual and group economic, intellectual, and cultural activities, all of which affect the economic and political fabric. From a long-range perspective, the feedback from tertiary effects may well prove to be the most enduring.

Structural conditions work against the U.S. information industries when they compete with the Japanese industries. Venture capital markets in the United States encourage the formation of small specialized companies, each of which often has a narrow product range. Conversely, MITI provides funds to large integrated Japanese firms in which no single product is vital to ultimate profitability. These integrated Japanese companies (both vendors and semiconductor suppliers) can use the strategy of lower prices to enter markets. As an example, a large integrated Japanese electronics firm was found by the International Trade Commission to have "dumped" its Klystron and traveling wave tubes, used in satellite communications, in the U.S. market. By pricing its tubes far below what the two small American suppliers could charge and below what it charged at home, the Japanese firm won the principal procurement rights from Communications Satellite Corporation (COMSAT); the survival of the two U.S. firms was jeopardized.

In the semiconductor industry, American firms have as their principal business the sale of semiconductor components and systems, while the Japanese digital semiconductor industry consists of large integrated firms. The Japanese firms have demonstrated in the past that they will use low prices to gain market entry. This pricing approach has been used in the 16K dynamic random-access memory (D-RAM) and the 64KD-RAM products.

POLICIES IN THE UNITED STATES, JAPAN, AND FRANCE

The birth, growth, and decline of industries has always been a cause of international tensions. Up to now, most international tensions arose from attempts to arrest the decline of industries. A further qualitative set of trade issues arises as we find industrial nations actively promoting their sunrise industries and developing countries seeking access to such industries. The information industries are coming to be regarded as the driving force in propelling our post-industrial society into a knowledge-intensive society.

Information has several unique attributes. In contrast to the finite nature of material resources, the value of information increases as it is used. Information is not depleted, but it may become obsolete. It is a basic factor of productive activity comparable with labor, capital, energy, or raw materials. The considerations of information transport, information access, and information processing form the basis for the information technology industries.

National industrial policy and public policy have played a stimulating role in the competitiveness of information industries in various countries. Japan and France are already committed to such nationally overseen programs governing the information industries. As would be expected, particular national policies vary according to national philosophy and goals as well as market and other economic conditions. Nonetheless, most policies have been characterized by attempts to provide R&D funds and to protect domestic industries against competition in general and against foreign competition in particular through protectionist procurement policies, restriction of foreign investment, and other more subtle non-tariff barriers. Countries have typically attempted to promote their industries via massive direct and indirect subsidies, including tax provisions and preferential loan treatment.

As might be expected, the results have been mixed. The lack of success in the development of state-supported information industries suggests the limits of state intervention in industries that form an integral part of an international marketplace, that are characterized by rapid change, and whose scope is not limited to a single sector in the economy.

Long-Term Outlook and Market Orientation

Countries with a long-term outlook and a well-established mechanism for establishing public policy regarding high-technology industries have had numerous advantages. The information industries are a good example of how important such factors really are.

Japan is the most effective country in implementing national information policies as a component of industrial policy. As a result of well-directed industrial policies toward certain knowledge-intensive industrial and consumer markets based on a careful comparative assessment of its industrial position, Japan has emerged as one of the world leaders in information industries. Unlike the United States, which has allowed market forces to dictate the direction of investment, the Japanese government has selected industries, allocated tasks, and promoted national champions or "winners," in consultation with industry and the banks ("administrative guidance"). Close attention is given to product gaps or weaknesses in the international marketplace that correspond—or may be made to correspond—to the Japanese comparative advantage.

However, such priorities and allocation of tasks is not necessarily sufficient. For example, the French have had an over-arching vision of the central role of information technology in the economy, but French firms and the French government have consistently failed to translate technological advances to the competitive marketplace, despite their possessing considerable technical and industrial expertise. The heavy hand of the French state and the lack of dynamism in the French market have limited the advancement of the French information industries. The much discussed gap between French and American—and now Japanese—industries has not been technological. Rather it relates to dependence on government orders, particularly telecommunications and the military, attitudes of distaste toward the competitive marketplace, a lack of entrepreneurial attitudes in the electronics industry, and dependence on foreign sources for advanced semiconductors.

Public Policy and Technological Change

As a result of vast technical changes since World War II in the United States and in most other countries, public policy has not kept pace with technology. The continuation of antediluvian regulations and outmoded policy frameworks in traditional areas and the absence of policy guidance in new areas have been major roadblocks to the emergence of information technology and the information industries. Furthermore, the complexity of information-based societies has led to certain issue clusters, which have not been appropriately addressed in national policies; national policies still focus on compartmentalized issues. The Japanese have in some cases addressed these issue clusters, but others have not.

The inhibiting role played by inappropriate public policy has been the most apparent in the telecommunications industry, although for different reasons in the United States and Western Europe. Modern technology has blurred traditional distinctions that current national communications policies are based upon. The merging of the communications and computer industries has raised numerous regulatory questions concerning competition versus "natural" monopolies; local versus regional, national, and international interests; social efforts to protect privacy versus economic considerations about efficiency; and national security objectives as opposed to efficiency and local interests.

Technological changes have made current policy approaches obsolete in most countries. In the United States, communications regulations are still primarily based on a meaningless separation of the computer and communications industries, although there have been some piecemeal changes—for example, the AT&T antitrust settlement and the dismissal of IBM's antitrust cases. The 1934 Communications Act, although much modified by the Federal Communications Commission (FCC), placed monopoly and national interests ahead of competitive and local interests. As a result, decisions in the United States have been fragmentary, inappropriate, and limiting.

Industries that were once analytically placed in either a regulated or nonregulated environment because of existing technological possibilities and public interests have now become competitors as a result of the complex and rapidly evolving changes in the structure of the information industries. AT&T was prohibited from competing in the computer field by the FCC's 1956 DOD–AT&T Consent Decree, which made an artificial distinction between computers and communications. [With the break-up of the Bell System in 1983, AT&T is now producing computers—and is competing head-on with IBM.]

In Europe and Japan, government-owned communications authorities continue to control communications services and investment. Competition is limited by protectionist procurement policies, subsidies, and other barriers in an attempt to provide a reliable infrastructure for national security, commercial, and consumer interests. Yet communications costs are high and service is often unreliable. In response to the new technological developments, most governments have merely widened their protectionist scope to incorporate the technologies in traditional terms, not recognizing the competitive issues involved and their possible economic benefits.

Policy approaches of governments continue to reside within a strictly national framework, despite the truly international character of the information industries. Growing numbers of international joint ventures—particularly between Japanese and European, and now Japanese and American, firms—indicate the limits of policies directed toward national industries. Despite the importance of technology transfer through international arrangements, foreign investment is frequently regulated and limited. Competition is still considered basically in domestic terms, although important competitive issues are usually between firms from different countries. In the United States, antitrust policy is aimed at domestic competition. Relevant markets and market shares continue to be defined in purely domestic terms. In Japan and Europe, although some joint ventures are blessed and encouraged for international competitive reasons, competitive policies frequently restrict the participation of foreign companies, especially American, in those domestic markets. For example, France refused to grant Digital Equipment Corporation a permit to establish a factory for minicomputers.

Political and Social Goals
versus Technological and Economic Goals

In the promotion of the information industries, there has frequently been confusion between political and social goals on one hand, and technical and economic goals on the other. Confusion often occurs because of (1) the general national importance of the information industries as a source of world economic and political power, and (2) the legitimacy of social goals, such as protection of privacy and national security objectives. Technological independence, which combines technical and political components, has been a common goal of governments at all economic levels. Generally, the extent of independence has been ill-conceived in relation to a country's resource endowment, especially in less developed countries. As a result, political objectives have undermined technical objectives. National interests of countries should be examined more closely, with the goal of obtaining the best technology available rather than of building a national industry for political reasons.

U.S. Public Policy for High-Technology Industries

It is time to raise the question of U.S. national industrial policy for high-technology. The complete disarray of public policy in the United States has had a negative impact on the international competitiveness of U.S. high-technology industries, particularly information technology. Lack of a coherent national policy plus certain structural constraints of the industry have served to erode the United States' industrial leadership.

A most damning indictment arose in June 1982 from the Office of Technology Assessment (OTA), which is in itself a high-technology watchdog for Congress. The OTA report cites the erosion of U.S. leadership in the civil space launch and satellite industry, and attributes this to the lack of clear, consistent, and sustained national and industrial objectives by the executive and legislative branches of the federal government. Conversely, the European Space Agency and also the Japanese government have developed national plans, supported by their respective governments and communications authorities.

International trade policies form an important subset to national policies. The market-oriented economy based on relatively free competition has stood the United States in good stead and its industrial leadership has prospered. However, American leadership must recognize that increasingly the high-technology sunrise industries are faced with international competitors backed by coherent national policies. Competition in international high-tech industries is not "pure" competition; it is strongly tainted by government intervention and support. The United States is obliged to strengthen its own high-technology industries seeking world markets, while maintaining its competitive, capitalistic structure.

U.S. international trade policy is presently a morass of dispersed responsibilities lodged with the Departments of Defense, Commerce, and Justice, the U.S. Trade Representative, the National Aeronautics and Space Administration (NASA), the Federal Communications Commission, the Office of Technology Assessment in Congress, and other entities. The Inter-Agency Committee on International Communications and Information Policy established on July 10, 1981, is a belated and insufficient attempt to coordinate U.S. responses to international bodies and international issues.

As a result, in the United States technology outpaces policy. The most glaring example is the FCC's attempts to come to grips with the technological convergence of telecommunications and computers. After several years of deliberations, the FCC issued the so-called Computer Inquiry I; this was immediately recognized as obsolete and inappropriate in attempting to separate telecommunications and computers. The FCC attempted again with Computer Inquiry II and was consistent in its technical approach, but the process became bogged down in adversarial and judicial proceedings. The FCC's problems arose out of the 1956 DOD–AT&T Consent Decree, which restricted AT&T to regulated communications businesses. [AT&T was unleashed to compete in the computer field through its Western Electric subsidiary in 1983, as part of the antitrust settlement; the full scope of that settlement remains unclear.]

Meanwhile, Siemens AG in Germany, Compagnie Générale Electricité and Thomson-CSF in France, Philips in the Netherlands, General Electric Company Limited in the United Kingdom, and Hitachi, Fujitsu, and Nippon Electric in Japan all have been active for years in implementing the equipment convergence of computers and communications. AT&T was restricted for the better part of three decades as to what products and business Western Electric could enter. The question of a regulated common carrier possibly subsidizing its equipment is a unique situation and does not appear to be the case for Western Electric.

Not only does the United States lack coherent national information industrial policies and related international trade policies, but a regulatory agency such as the FCC has great difficulty effectively dealing with the restrictions imposed by the Department of Justice.

Public Policy in France

The Giscard regime recognized that *télématique* (telecommunications and teleprocessing) and *bureautique* (office systems) were important to French internal development and export sales. In 1974 the French government forced the sale of the ITT (U.S.) and Ericsson (Swedish) telecommunications subsidiaries to Thomson-CSF and CGE, thus completing French control of the telecommunications industry. Only because IBM and Texas Instruments were too important to the French economy and because each had very strong management were the French prevented from gaining direct control of the computer and semiconductor industries in their country.

The French *télématique* product strategy was apparently to oblige the Postal, Telephone and Telegraph (PTT) agency to purchase large quantities of new communications terminals so as to achieve a low price and thus permit even larger export sales. Although the plans for the PTT proved to be overly ambitious, Matra and Thomson-CSF have developed low-cost workstations that incorporate a telephone, a video screen, and local intelligence. These workstations have been ordered in the United States in substantial quantities by Tymshare and GTE, which resell them to end users. French suppliers may be 12 to 18 months ahead of their principal American competitors; however, the two-step distribution is costly. If the two French companies shipped 25,000 terminals per year, the revenues would be approximately $10 million, which is modest in comparison with the French negative balance of trade in information products.

The same Giscard program also helped French industry to develop low-cost digital facsimile equipment. This, too, is being sold in the United States, and despite the two-step distribution appears to be an attractive device with several years of sales life; it will contribute only modestly to the French balance of trade.

Both terminal and facsimile equipment illustrate that French industry can be competitive in product design and manufacturing cost. These are not the problems. The government contracts have been superimposed on existing French industry without making this industry the focal point of a sustained and scientific, engineering, and export marketing program for the basic information sector.

The present French government has indicated that it considers high technology so important that it was considered a separate agenda point at the June 1982 economic summit at Versailles. The principal French thrust announced to date is a World Center for Microcomputers and Human Resources with the stated purpose of carrying the benefits of microcomputer technology to the Third World. This French effort was funded at $20 million in 1982 and far exceeds in funding any comparable laboratory in the United States. The French have recruited many of the best-known researchers, including leading Americans, for their Center. The Diebold Group's view is that the price of personal computers will decline so rapidly in the next several years that there is little that the French center will contribute to that development. United States and Japanese firms will provide opportunities for personal computation to large numbers of consumers, and even the developing countries will enjoy low prices.

The caliber and specialties of the research staff recruited by the French suggest that advanced and esoteric applications will be studied. What is not clear at this time is how successfully this Center will be coupled to French industry. Now that the French electronics industry has been nationalized, will they develop the marketing infrastructure that is essential to domestic and export sales of information products? With the exception of CII-Honeywell Bull, the French industrial electronics companies have limited experience selling to large numbers of small users.

Public Policy in Japan

Japanese and French policies remain profoundly different despite the fact that both countries have publicly announced that the information industries are the key to their national industrial policy. National industrial policy formulation has been ingrained in the Japanese government since the Meiji restoration. The Japanese, coordinated by MITI, have created a "vision of the 1980s" that is based on commercial exploitation (domestic products and exports) of the knowledge-intensive industries.

The distinguishing feature of all the Japanese "visions" is that they harness all development, product planning, marketing, and financing programs to clear *commercial* objectives. These plans have been drawn up in a concerted set of meetings with government, university, industry, and banking representatives who together forge an industry consensus.

The most recent MITI vision differs from previous plans in that it places emphasis on the "R" in R&D. The Japanese excel in product design, manufacturing, and quality control. Now they intend to be competitors in research, a more problematical task.

Through a series of MITI-sponsored meetings, the critical events are identified and direct funding and other forms of financial assistance are provided. The MITI funding is substantial and the programs are funded over a three- or four-year period. Apart from development funding, modest Japanese assistance programs are composed of a multitude of financial benefits or allowances which in aggregate make commercial success more possible.

Current and Proposed Development Policies

International trade policies have usually been centered on the support of declining industries. Recent efforts have dealt with international trade negotiation on the imports of European or Japanese steel into the U.S. market. These trade issues are exacerbated in economic recessions. The position of The Diebold Group is that it would be more productive for the national and international focus in international trade and public policy to concentrate at least as much effort on the sunrise industries, which are often based on high technology.

Several national programs have been successful and have contributed to international economic development. Perhaps the most successful initiative was the U.S. Congress passing the Communications Satellite Act of 1962.

This uniquely American initiative for structuring an advanced technology business led subsequently to an international consortium for satellite communications. The

Communications Satellite Corporation (COMSAT) blended launch vehicle (rocket) expertise and communications systems expertise, both of which were developed for defense or space agency purposes, with a private management structure. Technological innovations have continued in the past 20 years and will continue for the foreseeable future. Satellite communications will eventually have their most dramatic impact on communications in developing countries. Yet despite the pioneering efforts of the United States in satellites, the previously mentioned OTA report is very critical of the United States' present lack of clear national or commercial objectives in civilian space programs.

Another successful national implementation has been the Japanese integrated circuit project. Government agencies led by MITI and the Finance Ministry have provided the "administrative" guidance, hundreds of millions in financial support, and protection where necessary to foster the development of the computer industry and the Very Large-Scale Integrated Circuit (VLSIC) program for the semiconductor industry.

Through MITI, the Japanese government has recently launched its vision of a "fifth-generation" computer development program which will endure through the 1980s. This is a very ambitious goal, for it would incorporate artificial intelligence as well as the most advanced technology. Although the program is firmly under Japanese control, it has welcomed foreign participation. The British Department of Industry and American firms are observing with interest.

The United States has demonstrated that when government leadership decides on a major program requiring advanced technology, it can successfully mobilize immense resources. The audacious Apollo "Man-on-the-Moon" program was a major technological and political success. The material benefits to the world community are still, for the most part, indirect, and the medium-term direct benefits are probably not commensurate with the project's cost.

Given the immense technology and management resources resident in the United States, the question arises: Might not the United States identify programs or projects vital to its economy and society which are of national magnitude and importance? Such national projects should be possible in energy, biogenetics and health, and information technology, just to mention the most obvious. The first step could be the identification of a short list of such vital projects. Given that projects of national or worldwide importance can be identified, what mechanism does the United States have for national prioritization, coordination, and implementation?

The COMSAT experience is a very appealing example. Inspired by President John Kennedy, the initiative called for a government-mandated commercial enterprise to promote U.S. leadership in satellite communications. Established by Congress in the Communications Satellite Act of 1962, the Communications Satellite Corporation— COMSAT—is still very successful; it continues to provide world technological leadership and is increasingly involved in competitive and profitable ventures. The cost to the taxpayer has been nominal and the entire world has benefited. COMSAT was unique in that it brought together two industries, one of which was completely dependent on the U.S. government for its development.

Could the United States or other industrial countries duplicate the COMSAT experience in other industries? The first step to answering this question requires expert analysis of each of those industries.

The second step is the analysis of the projects and industries to develop in each a "COMSAT-like" approach that would be congenial to private industry and yet limit the cost to the taxpayer. This concept should be considered for projects of vital national interest. Such projects are not the equivalent of a coherent national program, but they could be effective and would represent the best that the United States could accomplish in peacetime, given the present national economic and political ethos.

International Diffusion of Technology

In developing public policies for the information industries, we must recognize the increasing internationalization of those industries. Such internationalization, with its attendant diffusion of technology, will require shared research and development and, in some situations, joint manufacturing, marketing, and services. Both American and Japanese firms have recognized the difficulty of penetrating each other's industrial markets and therefore there is an increasing trend toward joint marketing and services arrangements. The arrangements are not symmetrical because the U.S. exports technology while Japan exports products.

We expect that technological developments will continue to outpace the evolution of public policies and regulatory agencies. Even the most responsive U.S. government agencies are handicapped by the litigious nature of the adversary position in a quasi-legal environment. The best work of the Federal Communications Commission and its staff is often thwarted by the atmosphere in which it must operate. The structure of the semiconductor industry suggests some need for shared research, which the Department of Justice has recognized since 1980 as beneficial.

In the United States, the annual R&D effort from all sources is about $80 billion. Private industry provides over 50 percent of R&D funds, with the federal government funding most of the remainder. The DOD provides approximately one third of the total or $25 billion. A small fraction of this is seed money for fundamental and basic research; most is for the ad hoc development of military-specific products. Contrary to what most European experts believe, the U.S. defense and space programs provide only occasional direct benefits or commercial spinoffs to industry.

Military objectives often impose rigid design specifications that are not appropriate for commercial products. In almost every instance, the R&D effort demonstrated product feasibility, but several important steps remained in order for the design to be successfully adapted to commercial products.

The direct fallout of commercial products from the Department of Defense or NASA has been limited. There are few examples as direct as Boeing's modeling its original 707 jet aircraft design after the Air Force KC135 refueling tanker.

On the other hand, the indirect contributions from the Department of Defense or NASA projects have been substantial, and include digital computer designs, digital communications devices, and medical electronics. (Indirect fallout occurs when a commercial product utilizes the same basic technological research that was done for the military product, but with substantial modifications necessary to adapt the product for commercial use.)

Forecasting the evolution of the commercialization of scientific breakthroughs is a hazardous activity. For example, few if any, foresaw the parallel development of laser optics and semiconductor materials that led to the development of semiconductor lasers and semiconductor detectors. These electro-optical devices will have a profound impact on future telecommunications and information processing systems.

The most poignant example of the contrast between the U.S. government's support of industry and Japanese programs is evident in the key semiconductor industry. The Department of Defense had its Very High-Speed Integrated Circuit (VHSIC) program and the Japanese had their Very Large-Scale Integrated Circuit (VLSIC) program. The DOD VHSIC program was directed toward the development of electronic circuits that would operate in difficult military environmental conditions—including nuclear war. In this $314 million program, many small contracts for a few millions of dollars each were spread among a number of U.S. semiconductor firms, with considerable emphasis on developing "second sources" or multiple suppliers. Significantly, several of the principal U.S. firms chose *not* to participate in the VHSIC program.

In contrast, the VLSIC program of the Japanese was directed toward commercial applications, and $300 million was divided among a small number of large integrated

Japanese firms that have competent R&D departments and are funded for both the heavy capital costs and for the aggressive pricing strategy in market entry—which is characteristic of the integrated Japanese electronic firms.

A second example is the DOD requirement for a high-tensile strength fiber-optics cable for use in missile programs. The acknowledged world leader in fiber optics is Corning. Japanese firms, however, were willing to make development efforts in order to gain a market share. This fiber-optics example raises several critical issues—national security, reciprocity of market entry, long-term U.S. industrial interests, and U.S. employment, all of which should be weighed before a decision is made. In this case, we have the DOD's immediate needs, plus whatever narrow political pressures can be brought to bear by the U.S. industry, as the determinants of national policy in a critical technology. The United States does not have an adequate mechanism, apart from ad hoc DOD or executive judgments, to deal with such issues.

ACTION ISSUES

Establishing Public Policies in the United States

In democratic countries, effective national public policies must have substantial support from the opinion makers and the informed public. Therefore, it is necessary to raise public consciousness regarding the importance of the high-technology industries to the economic success and personal enrichment in the knowledge-intensive post-industrial society.

Given the present high-decibel level of discussion in the United States regarding deregulation of communications and the AT&T settlement, it is unlikely that the information industries can come to an agreement about the technological implications for the future. It may be essential to appoint a blue-ribbon panel to develop positions that would reflect a general consensus of the business opportunities and social enrichment, which should be the twin objectives of U.S. industrial policy. There is always the danger in creating such a panel that technical developments could continue to outpace the panel's understanding and comprehension.

We previously discussed the COMSAT model. A necessary early step in policy formulation is the examination of the operative conditions of both the COMSAT model and the Japanese MITI-industry relationship in order to ascertain what is most appropriate for the United States. The COMSAT-MITI analysis would be most useful in formulating possible mechanisms for U.S. policy.

An example of a project of national importance that could be structured along the COMSAT-MITI lines is a portable personal communications equipment capability that would enable individuals to connect to local, national, and international networks. Using a small hand-held device, not unlike Dick Tracy's wristwatch, individuals could transmit voice or data or both. A portable personal communications project, while representing formidable technical problems, is not constrained by major systems engineering tasks. The magnitude of the project lies more in the development of receiver sensitivity. Transmitter power would be limited by health and technical considerations.

Why should the government become involved when major electronics firms are aware of both the challenge and the opportunity? Such a project is a political opportunity to raise the public's awareness of technology, in the same vein as the first Apollo moon landing. Demonstrable progress should be possible while the ultimate usefulness of the technology has almost universal appeal.

Such a program would be outlined by the best telecommunications talent in the United States. The critical research paths would be identified and funded to a modest degree at universities or other nonprofit institutions. The results could be made available on a royalty basis to American industries. Collaborative research by private industry could well be an alternate to some or all of government funding. Once beyond the difficult research phase the project would become market driven. This proposed American approach is based on government involvement only in identifying the key research tasks and providing, at most, research seed money.

International connections would no doubt be hindered by political obstacles. Almost all foreign telecommunications authorities are state owned and are not necessarily market driven. French telecommunications authorities are notorious for favoring their local equipment suppliers. The goal of the U.S. public policy would be to encourage substantial export revenues for domestic suppliers while recognizing that the individual foreign telecommunications authorities would probably utilize their monopoly position in negotiating with multiple American suppliers. The U.S. industry would, in effect, confront foreign government cartels and monopolies.

U.S. Public Policy Issues

Can U.S. leadership in the information sector be sustained by traditional responses to the broad front of other purposeful government-directed efforts to challenge that leadership? The uncoordinated, pluralistic, market-driven U.S. business environment has served American information industries well in the past. Has it become inappropriate for the new competitive conditions of the 1980s and beyond?

Government policies that were created during one era in the United States are being applied to another. Technological change, competitive and economic shifts, and the increased role of governments in industrial policies for the information sector may well render the traditional approach inadequate. Policies are often contradictory and generally inappropriate. But what is the alternative? How far can a coordinating mechanism go without losing the free market dynamism and innovation that have served the United States so well in the past?

The country would derive the greatest advantages by promoting its strongest feature, its market-driven economy, rather than by adopting forms that are alien to it. Because the structure and attitudes of U.S. business and political communities encourage confrontation rather than cooperation, a policy modeled completely on the Japanese system would clearly be inappropriate.

Nonetheless, there is currently a need in the United States for coordinated public policy in the information sector based on the appreciation of the central importance of the information sector for the future of the entire economy. The central policy issues include the following:

1. *Establishing appropriate and consistent regulations to allow development of the new technology.* Technological development has made existing regulatory guidelines and structures inappropriate in numerous ways. As a result, policy has been formulated in a piecemeal fashion. For example, the settlement between the Justice Department and AT&T has changed Bell from a telephone company to an information company. Recent technological changes have led to many questions and few answers:

- How should interests in competition be balanced against the need for regulation, particularly given new changes in technology that mean that computers and telecommunications industries and services are virtually indistinguishable?
- Is the theory of natural monopoly in communications still relevant under current technological conditions?
- How can the government reconcile its interest in regulating the communications industry with its other interest in encouraging the competitive aspects of the industry? For example, the Department of Defense opposed breaking up AT&T on national security grounds, while the Justice Department and FCC decisions concerning the industry have emphasized competition.

- How should local needs be balanced with regional, national, or international needs?
- Will the new communications industries be regulated? If so, which agencies will have the primary regulatory powers? Furthermore, how will communications charges be established if the industry becomes highly competitive, if local jurisdictions are given regulatory power, and if sophisticated communications permit elaborate routing procedures that cut across regulatory boundaries?
- How will the AT&T settlement affect competition and regulation in telecommunications?

The domestic treatment of industries has a direct effect on their international competitiveness and will affect foreign imports. Similar types of issues are being debated throughout the world, as technological change is leading to a rethinking of traditional attitudes and approaches elsewhere.

2. *Deciding whether a model code for the United States should be created regarding laws or regulatory policies in information areas, such as satellites, cable, videotex, and other information products.* One solution to the regulatory problems resulting from technological developments could be the formulation of a model code. The code could cover overlapping areas of jurisdiction and laws, competitive issues, and standards among stages. Such an approach could be adopted for the international community as well in order to reduce the confusion and other problems created by widely different approaches. The standards

issues are addressed by the Consultative Committee for
International Telephone and Telegraph (CCITT) in international forums.

*3. Formulating U.S. antitrust guidelines, based on a
review of the impact to date of laws and regulations.* We
need innovation-oriented antitrust guidelines, based on a
review of the effect antitrust policy (as practiced in the
United States) has had on the development of information-
sector industries. The study should weigh the anti-compet-
itive aspects of certain practices against their effect on a
more viable information sector. For example, was the 1956
Consent Decree that kept AT&T out of the computer
business short-sighted or did it encourage competition that
would not have otherwise occurred? Similarly, in the 13-
year IBM case, was IBM prevented from increasing its
competitiveness because of the pending court decision or
did more competition result from the case?

In view of technological developments and competitive
conditions, antitrust concepts for relevant markets, competition, and market share need to be reconsidered. Although U.S. industries are highly competitive in the domestic market, there is intense international competition.
Yet traditional antitrust policy in the United States defines
relevant markets and other competitive concerns in strictly
domestic terms.

Antitrust policy could have a very positive effect on
research and development in the information sector. The
competitive success of these industries, both domestic and
international, is based on the ability to continue building a
technological research base as well as conducting applied
research. However, with semiconductor and certain infor-

mation technology products, it is questionable whether U.S. companies have the resources to match the efforts of foreign government-supported integrated industries in the future. This is particularly important as these industries become more research- and capital-intensive. The leaders of a new joint research effort in the United States feel that the funding, manpower, and range of technology required for the country to maintain its competitiveness in the semiconductor field are beyond the capability of most individual U.S. companies.

Yet current antitrust laws may be an impediment to effective competition. Research policy is considered to be an important element in the overall competitive process, but joint research frequently raises antitrust questions. The complexity of antitrust attitudes toward joint research has frequently discouraged such activities from taking place. In recognition of this problem, President Carter directed the Justice Department to produce a guide to its antitrust policies upon the conclusion of the White House Domestic Policy Review of Industrial Innovation. Accordingly, the Justice Department issued the "Antitrust Guide Concerning Research Joint Ventures" in November 1980. This was a positive first step, but the subject requires more fundamental examination. Several efforts for joint research arrangements by U.S. firms in direct response to the Japanese challenge have been evident recently. However, the antitrust implications are not totally clear.

William Norris, Chairman of Control Data Corp., has sponsored one such initiative called Microelectronics and Computer Technology Corporation (MCC) that lets producers pool research activities under university auspices.

Based in Austin, Texas, MCC is headed by former CIA director Bobby Inman, who has been specifically charged with the difficult task of steering the company away from antitrust action.

4. Examining U.S. tax policies that would promote new industries and decrease their risk. In contrast to Japan, where tax policy is one of the strongest incentives for information industries, U.S. tax policy for innovation is not a priority. The unique needs of the high-technology information industries are just beginning to be addressed here. Tax policy can and should play a more positive and central role in the encouragement of U.S. competitiveness. A thorough examination of these issues should be undertaken.

There are several areas where tax policy can promote innovation through the free market mechanism. Depreciation allowances and depreciation periods should reflect the fact that many of the industries are characterized by low profitability and short product cycles. In addition, tax allowances for research and development are needed as incentives. Computer equipment and software suppliers have benefited from the R&D tax credit and accelerated depreciation sections of the Economic Recovery Tax Act of 1981, but more measures along these lines are needed.

In addition, tax benefits for educational purposes could lead to the increased education of citizens about the value of the information sector. Apple Computer encountered problems in obtaining tax credits for educational donations of its products. And ironically, one of the main casualties of the IBM antitrust case were the universities and schools which had been receiving large educational discounts from

IBM. Tax benefits could also encourage the much-needed training of additional personnel for these industries.

The programming (software) industry faces potential problems because it is taxed differently from the hardware industry in the United States and several other countries. Programs are increasingly being viewed as a commodity in themselves. More than 30 states currently tax programs, and several foreign countries have adopted such provisions.

Finally, current tax laws and proposals that affect the United States' competitive position overseas should be considered in the context of promoting and developing the information industries. The issues of foreign tax credits and DISC (pending the outcome of international negotiations) should be assessed.

5. Studying U.S. patent and copyright laws to determine what changes would better promote innovation. The development of new technology and products and the transformation of old technology and products have resulted in a host of complex patent and copyright questions. Because established policy and policy structures are inadequate when it comes to resolving many of the new leading issues, policy questions are more frequently resolved in the courts, which are inappropriate for the purpose. Decisions are segmented, inconsistent, and frequently ill-guided in developing national technology policy. This area has an important effect on U.S. domestic competition, the success of foreign companies in the U.S. market, and the U.S. position abroad.

Software sales provides the best example of the problems. Computer programs will soon become one of the most important growth fields; programming costs currently account for approximately 65 percent of total user costs. The expected astronomical growth in personal computers [which exceeded $6 billion in 1983] will lead to an explosion in the demand for software programs. A variety of program packages permits the owner of a single personal computer to undertake limitless tasks.

Despite the importance of programming, patent and copyright protection is poor and programs are very easy to duplicate. The Apple Computer Company has estimated that it loses 10 to 50 percent of its potential program business through illegal program distribution. This problem has intensified with the appearance of new "decipher" programs, which can copy most programs within 15 minutes. The lack of protection has been an important deterrent to advances in programming.

The history of protection for programs is limited and fragmentary. Initially, programs were provided free to customers to promote the sale of computers in the early days of the industry. It was not until 1968 that the U.S. Court of Customs and Patent Appeals ruled that "truly novel" computer programs are to be considered inventions and are therefore patentable. However, the U.S. Copyright Act was not amended until December 1980 to cover computer program protection. Now users are permitted to copy programs for "archival purposes" only, but there is little enforcement. Engineers are designing "booby-traps" to prevent their programs from being illegally used or pirated, but these efforts are limited.

The issue has a great international significance as well because patent and copyright protection abroad is also poor. The U.S. Office of the Special Trade Representative estimates that 21 countries do not have protection and, as a result, infringements occur. In addition, France and the United Kingdom provide export subsidies to their domestic programming industries. In Brazil, the government is nationalizing the program industry.

U.S. policymakers should examine the domestic and international aspects of impediments to program development. Similar issues arise in connection with numerous other information industries and products, such as videotape recorders and various information services.

6. Adopting trade policies that emphasize freer market access abroad and reduce the penetration of U.S. information industry markets due to "unfair" competition. One of the main obstacles to the continued strength of the American information sector is the protectionism abroad of key information industries, particularly in the communications field, which restricts U.S. export opportunities. A related challenge is the penetration of U.S. markets by foreign industries that have had the advantages of strong government support. Such activities are incompatible with U.S. interests in maintaining a policy of free trade. As part of its overall public policy to encourage the emergence of a strong information sector, U.S. policymakers should adopt an active trade policy through existing trade bodies, including GATT and the OECD.

There are indications that the concern for selected high-technology trade is now understood. The Administration is considering taking "unfair trade" actions against several other countries for complaints of dumping and subsidies of information industries. Reciprocity bills concerning high-technology industries abroad have started to appear on Capitol Hill. The Semiconductor Industry Association has urged that Congress adopt legislation authorizing the United States to negotiate with other countries for freer market access for high-technology goods and services and investment. In addition, the Senate Finance Committee's international trade subcommittee has heard testimony concerning the problems that computer companies face abroad in maintaining majority ownership. This is particularly a problem for young export-oriented companies. In order to defuse trade tensions between the United States and Japan over U.S. market access in Japan and Japanese market penetration in the United States, the two countries agreed to a subcabinet-level working group. The United States apparently hopes to raise these issues in appropriate international forums as well.

7. *Indentifying potential areas of demand imparted by information technology that are currently regulated or restricted.* As a result of legal custom, regulations, contracts, or tradition, the development of numerous industry sectors are restricted, despite the availability of technology whose applications would transform those industries.

Banking is one of the best examples. Through the application of information technology, the nature of banking itself has changed. Electronic funds transfer (EFT) and automated teller machines (ATMs) have meant that money can be shifted globally within a few seconds. The interstate and international capabilities of banking have far exceeded the regulatory bounds. Further, the development of new financial services by unregulated concerns has placed banks at a disadvantage. How meaningful and appropriate is current regulation under these conditions? In addition, the question of what constitutes a bank is no longer easily answered because of computer linkages, electronic credit facilities, ATMs, and other innovations in the information sector.

Technology has made an international electronic stock market possible. Interconnection of the various markets could actually enhance the efficiency of the marketplace by instantaneously matching up supply and demand. A computerized network would provide a clearinghouse for the market.

Other examples include the legal questions surrounding the need for an original document versus the efficiency of providing a facsimile document, in light of today's rapid electronic transmission capabilities. Workplace safety rules may change appreciably when robots become a greater part of the workplace.

Technology is changing education as well, but there is resistance to these changes among teachers who do not understand the technology and are worried about their job security. Computer technology is increasingly becoming part of curricula. Finally, the nature of publishing is changing with the use of electronic transmission, but regulations still regard the media in traditional terms.

8. *Promoting information technology industries through education aid.* Policymakers need to consider what role, if any, public policy should play in information education. Should government, either at the local, state, or federal level, become involved with the issue? Should it offer companies incentives to educate the population about the importance of the information sector? The significance of

the sector to the U.S. economy suggests that the government should adopt some measures.

9. *Comparing the free market policies of the United States with two free market exceptions: national security and regulatory interests.* Since the Reagan Administration took office, "national security" has been cited more frequently to support restrictive actions toward the export and import of dual-use technology, as well as to support certain major domestic policy questions.

The Administration has adopted Operation Exodus in the Customs Service to prevent critical U.S. technology from reaching the Soviet Union. The Japanese company Fujitsu was not awarded the contract for the Northeast Corridor fiber optics project ostensibly on the grounds of national security. Secretary of Defense Caspar Weinberger argued that splitting up AT&T would not be in the American national security interest because of the need for a unified, reliable communications infrastructure.

The United States is not well-served if the government restricts the export of technology that the Soviet Union can purchase elsewhere. If the government relimits the U.S. export of advanced microchips, the Soviet Union will probably be able to buy them from Japanese or other firms. The Administration is attempting to solve the problem by placing pressure on U.S. allies to revise their guidelines for technology exports to the Soviet Union. The United States has pressed Germany to ban its sales of high-grade silicon to the Soviet Union, because it can be used to make chips in the guidance system of the Russian SS-20 missiles. As technology increases, there will be increased conflict between the national security and commercial interests of the country in this area.

In addition, the role of the government in the protection of citizens' right to privacy must be weighed against the advantages accruing from the free flow of information. Health, work-related, and other types of data have been the most frequently discussed issues in connection with the right to privacy. Adequate safeguards in these areas must be found, but the positive benefits of information technology should not be restricted.

Conclusions for the United States

The United States should attempt to formulate a coherent and well-integrated policy within its market-driven economy along the lines and the issues suggested. Any policy should recognize the dynamic features and international diffusion of the technology. In addition, policy should address the adjustment problems that are taking place as the economy shifts from traditional industries to the high-technology industries. Education, employment, and retraining issues will present major challenges for those who embark on a more comprehensive study of the public policy problems for this sector.

PUBLIC POLICY ISSUES FOR OTHER ADVANCED INDUSTRIAL NATIONS

Public policy agenda for other advanced industrial nations is different from that of the United States in that it is manifested in the costs of the protection and promotion of the information sector through active government intervention. The central issue is to weigh benefits of protection and promotion of the information sector against competitive costs of those policies to the economy and to society. National goals should be examined very carefully in the context of priorities. Is it more important to have domestic information industries at all costs or are there other strategies to be followed to establish a competitive information economy?

Costs and Benefits of Protectionism

Political goals are frequently confused with technical goals. Technological independence has been a typical goal of information policies, but it has been defined and sought in an inappropriate manner. As a result, political objectives have often undermined technical objectives. The strongest national interest of these countries lies in obtaining superior and applicable technology and applying it throughout the economy. The goals of developing a domestic industry should be closely weighed against the resources available to promote it and an appreciation of the determinants of its success. National strategies should reflect a country's comparative advantage. In addition, they should be based on the recognition of the country's role as a cooperative member of the international community.

Protectionism through government-owned monopolies. In Europe and Japan, the governments own the Postal, Telephone and Telegraph (PTT) agencies in order to regulate communications services and to provide a reliable infrastructure for national security and commercial and consumer interests. These objectives are generally not satisfied because the overriding goal of the governments is to protect its domestic companies, even if that means that the best technical equipment will not be used. For example, a telephone call from Paris to New York costs two times more than a call from New York to Paris; the difference is a factor of three from the Federal Republic of Germany. Even intra-European phone rates are costly because of PTT policies, and European businesses and consumers bear the brunt of the costs.

Government-owned monopolies have frequently given preference to political rather than economic considerations, but political benefits must be weighed against economic costs. Is the restriction on competition artificial? Would the domestic industries actually be stronger if competition were allowed? Alternatively, if deregulation took place, would the communications infrastructure be unreliable? The issue of standards could become very important. Another problem would be the incompatibility of products, which already exists among rival videotex and facsimile products.

Government telecommunications procurement policies are the most important trade barrier. Market access is generally permitted only to national telecom suppliers through preferential purchasing arrangements. This is particularly important to countries whose telecommunications industries are export oriented. Public telephone equipment comprises roughly 50 percent of the world market for telecommunications equipment of all types, yet most of these markets are closed to imports.

In France, the power of the PTT is unrivaled. Giscard's DGT (Direction Générale des Télécommunications) limited the role of foreign suppliers to modernize the French communications network. Protectionist procurement policies are applied to intra-European trade as well. The European Economic Community is currently attempting to convince governments to open their trade, but this has been a sore point in the commission. In Japan, despite the 1980 three-year bilateral agreement to permit U.S. suppliers to compete with Japanese suppliers for the Japanese market, procurement for NTT is limited to Japanese-owned companies, with only minor exceptions. Motorola was placed on NTT's approved supplier list for mobile paging equipment and ROLM for PBXs, but observers are skeptical about meaningful changes.

Performance requirements, including standards and designs and national content, are used to keep foreign goods out of the markets. In the United Kingdom, proposed applications for connection to British Telecom must pass the scrutiny of the British Standards Institute and then the British Electrical Approval Board. In France, domestic product content is monitored closely.

Telecommunications rates and rate increases are based on considerations other than costs in order to restrict private networks, to promote domestic data processing, and to promote public data communications networks. What are the costs to users versus the competitive benefits for local firms? The restriction on private lines affecting international communications is found in Japan and throughout the European community. In some cases, increased tariffs, which are the means of regulation, provide increased revenues for the PTTs. In general, local industries are promoted, but what are the disadvantages to the users versus the revenue gains to the PTTs? Does the restriction in data flow discourage foreign investment?

Restricting data processing functions. Much discussion has taken place on the question of trans-border data flows. For example, the Canadian government has recommended that data processing be performed solely within the country. The Canadian Banking Act of 1980 requires that banks operating in Canada keep and process all data concerning a bank customer in Canada. Do such regulations discourage foreign investment? What are the costs of investments as opposed to the benefits for the protection of local industries?

Promoting industries through government assistance. Most European countries and Japan provide their information industries with substantial financial incentives to promote development. These countries need to consider whether the assistance has helped or hindered the industries' development, and whether the industries are more or less competitive because of it. Are the political objectives worth the cost?

Selecting national champions or winners for government assistance. France picked computers as its "national champion" in the 1960s and 1970s. Mitterrand has also targeted the information sector for special development assistance. In Japan, there are particular products that are selected for government aid, as well as certain industries. Does a sectoral approach distort the economy? Does it depend on the type of sectoral assistance given? What are the disadvantages of selecting the wrong winner?

Tariffs. The European community maintains a tariff of 17

percent on integrated circuits and refuses to negotiate the levels to protect its industry and to prevent additional U.S. and Japanese imports. What are the costs of protection for the Europeans? The Japanese recently reduced their tariffs on integrated circuits to 4 percent, as did the United States.

Taxing information. The United Kingdom places a 4 percent duty and 8 percent value-added tax (VAT) on all microfilm documents and publications imported from non-Community countries. France has considered imposing a tax on information similar to a tax on imports or exports, but it has not adopted one.

Regulating foreign investment. Canada, Belgium, Brazil, Germany, and Switzerland place restrictions on commercial visas that limit outside firms' abilities to market and maintain their services. In addition, there are other discriminatory regulations that make it difficult for qualified people to work in the country. Finally, foreign investment or foreign ventures are often flatly prohibited.

PUBLIC POLICY ISSUES FOR DEVELOPING COUNTRIES

Developing countries face situations in which they would like to take advantage of the new information technologies to improve their standards of life through telecommunications changes and the use of other high-technology items. They also face the issue of specialization in information technology to build their economies. Numerous countries have already made key public policy decisions on these matters. Have the decisions been a mistake or of benefit? What can we learn from these experiences?

Appropriate Technology for Less Developed Countries

Several Third World countries have skipped a stage of the telecommunications process by adopting satellite technology rather than constructing a terrestrial long-distance communications infrastructure. India has already launched its own satellites to provide nationwide communication. Indonesia is developing a satellite communications system as well. Do these countries need the most advanced technologies? What should the criteria be? These are fertile areas for public policy study.

Should less developed countries attempt to develop an information product sector? With the large economic requirement of creating and sustaining information industries, countries should be very careful in establishing policies to promote domestic industries. Mexico and Brazil have adopted protectionist policies to promote the development of local industries. In Mexico, the rapidly expanding market has been restricted as the government is trying to build up a domestic industry. The government has informed foreign manufacturers to either produce in Mexico under certain conditions or to leave the country. Brazil has followed similar policies for similar reasons. However, in Brazil, the business community has complained that it must utilize outdated equipment that costs more than equivalent foreign-made items. The government has responded that a period of adjustment is necessary before the industry becomes competitive. Are these appropriate industries to be developing with limited resources? Will there be economic costs that will undermine technical goals, similar to the earlier French example in computers?

Policymakers in the developing countries should carefully consider their comparative advantage and develop industries on the basis of that advantage. A potential growth area for developing countries is software, which is labor intensive. Countries must learn how to take advantage of the growing software market.

Information and Political Issues

Many developing countries have actively pushed for a politically oriented New World Information Order in the areas of journalism, satellite agreements, and other areas. What are the economic and political costs and benefits of this issue? How are they to be viewed by the political authorities in the developing countries?

Other Issues for Consideration

There are several other areas that should be studied:

1. Do discriminatory trade practices hurt developing countries more than they help? Regulation of foreign investment, import protection, and export promotion are the main examples.
2. The cost of politicizing issues is high. How do countries separate legitimate technological and economic concerns from political objectives?

3. Citizens' right to privacy must be protected while industry reaps the economic benefits of the unimpeded flow of information.

CONCLUSION

The purpose of this analysis has been to illustrate the kinds of economic problems posed by the information technology industry and to highlight a few of the new policy questions that must be addressed.

In the determination of competitiveness and industrial policy for the information sector, public policy does make a difference, as we have seen by the various examples above. Government policy can have an impact that is positive, negative, or both. Even the lack of an explicit government policy can affect the development of the industries, as has happened in the United States. The precise relation between government policy and particular information industries is not well understood, and this chapter has merely suggested the starting points for a thorough discussion.

As has already been emphasized, the public policy agenda should vary for each country. The current American tendency to point to Japan and to try to produce some pale policy copy can lead only to disaster!

Every country needs to study both methodically and opportunistically the role of its public policy in shaping the information industries, since those industries are assuming increasing importance in the world's economies and, indeed, the quality of life. Based on the experiences of others, each country needs to develop policies that accommodate and enhance its progress of future technological growth. Although public policies for the information sector have existed since the computer industry developed, there has never been a thorough study of the role of public policy in the competitive success of the information industries. What is needed now is an integrated look at the problems of competitiveness, with domestic and international factors carefully weighed.

Chapter 3

INTERNATIONAL BUSINESS IN THE INFORMATION AGE

Information technology is becoming an international battleground. Leadership has generally been measured in terms of the suppliers of the technology: the industries that deliver computers and communications. However, an often overlooked factor is the user of the technology. The real test of whether a society will flourish in our increasingly information-intensive social and economic environment is how well that society can and will use information to capitalize on technological change.

This chapter is based on John Diebold's testimony in evidence to the All-Party Committee on Information Technology at the House of Commons in London, on April 17, 1980.

As the rapid pace of technological change is bringing about fundamental changes in our social and economic structures, it is not surprising that the information arena is becoming something of an international battleground. The lines are sometimes drawn unintentionally, as in those cases where a genuine effort to protect individual privacy by strictly regulating data flow across borders operates in practice as a non-tariff barrier.

The key to a flourishing society and economy in this age of information will be what I call the "demand side"—how well people can and will use information technology to adjust to and capitalize upon the new opportunities that already surround us. Ownership of information delivery systems capabilities—the "supply side"—will very likely continue to be an important comparative advantage for those economies that have leadership or near-leadership positions.

Our priority should be the creation of conditions that ensure that users of information systems have available to them the very best information infrastructure—computing capacity, data communications capability, and depth in educational and training facilities—in the world.

Technology has brought us to the threshold of a new wave of opportunities for using information in virtually all human pursuits. As the generation and use of information accounts for an increasingly significant part of the economic activity of industrial culture, policy should be aimed at maximizing the prospects for use patterns to take full advantage of the newly created possibilities.

Nationalistic policies can threaten full realization of the benefits of the inherently international information technology industries. Unfortunately, and predictably, many multi-national corporations are giving up economies of scale, flexibility, and other potential benefits by defensively decentralizing data processing by country, specifically to minimize business risks in the present uncertain environment.

THE DEMAND SIDE

I would like to begin by focusing on the user side of our information economy. It is important to understand that technological advances are rapidly changing the industry structures, the pattern of operation and use, and the user interfaces associated with information systems. To appreciate the implications of these changes we must look not only at information systems suppliers, but at how and where information is used in our economic systems.

How Information Is Used

The technology-driven convergence of data processing and telecommunications is rapidly creating a broad range of possibilities for electronic delivery systems, which will lead to basic changes in our social and economic structures. The prospects for cheap and ubiquitous terminals in the office and in the home, the fast-evolving new delivery capabilities associated with computers and communications services, and the potential for automating existing and new data bases are combining to give birth to a new generation of opportunities to use and leverage information.

As full electronic capability becomes economically feasible for business and the home, the possibility arises that a significant part of what today involves "going to the office" and "going shopping" can be accomplished from any place where there is a terminal.

From the standpoint of information suppliers, the potential for substitution requires understanding how the new electronic delivery systems can relate to what business and consumer users need. This might range from automating and consolidating funds transfer, office systems, and cost-saving environmental and security systems to supplementing (or even replacing) newspapers and other published materials with electronically distributed information that has an on-demand printing option.

With the advances that are currently being predicted in hardware technology, from X-ray lithography to superconductor systems, hardware is becoming increasingly like a commodity. The mind boggles when one thinks of prospects for commercial Josephson Junction superconductor systems with price and performance improvements measured in orders of magnitude beyond present capabilities! Value-added industries (with the profit economics that they entail) in what have been thought of up to now as information supplier industries are shifting to end-user-focused software.

From the standpoint of business users, competitive success will depend more and more on understanding the elements of customers' needs, on being able to discern potential substitutions for present businesses deriving from advances in delivery systems, and on creatively resegmenting markets.

Generally it will be important to recognize early the impact of the fast-moving technology on research and development (for example, sophisticated computer modeling), on production (users will be able to customize their purchases), on marketing (direct marketing, including interaction with customers via on-line electronic systems), on distribution, and so forth.

From the standpoint of consumers, individuals will soon have the capability to optimize the allocation of their time and personal resources in the face of inflation and scarce energy, to use greatly expanded educational resources more effectively and to improve their quality (if we can overcome the institutional barriers), to extend their personal reach, and undoubtedly to improve the quality of life in many other dimensions of human endeavor.

Creating a User-Friendly Environment

Information-related goods and services already account for a significant part of the economic activity of advanced industrial culture. However, to fully grasp the dimensions of the opportunities that are before us requires new economic measurements and classifications. In considering how to develop policies and investment incentives that will lead to capitalizing on these opportunities (which are inherently international in scope), we will have to think deeply about how to promote a user-friendly environment. Such an environment would be one where the conditions and infrastructures controlling the reach of human interactions and the flows of information are flexible and fluid enough to keep pace with the technology-enabled new possibilities.

Although narrowly defined information industries by themselves are not a trivial part of industrial economies, it is when we make broad-brush efforts to analyze the growing use of information resources by economies as a whole that we discover the most startling impacts of the information society. More than 40 to 50 percent of American economic activity is information related. (Figures like these are derived partly from the work of The Diebold Group, partly from the Harvard Program on Information Resources Policy, from Marc Porat's work on the information economy, and from other sources. Our assumptions and definitions relate to the production, processing, and distribution of information goods and services—including computers, communications, books, telecommunications, the media, education, R&D, various business services, and so on. We also include information services produced by non-information firms for internal consumption, including management, secretarial support, various kinds of functional support, and so on.)

Use is generally in very preliminary stages of sophistication, and primarily focused on *how* a process is achieved, rather than *what* is done. Even so, the "how" is far from being fully exploited. For example, the former head of a major retail firm recently remarked that he was not aware of a single large retail company in the world which even today has fully automated inventory control, although the technology to do so has been available for years.

In my firm's research and management consulting practice, it has become increasingly clear that economic definitions and measurements that worked quite well for thinking about manufacturing are not especially useful for thinking about today's information technologies. We believe that some newer concepts are necessary to fully grasp the opportunities that are open to us. Productivity measurements, for example, need to be re-thought generally, but especially so in order to understand the forces that come to bear in information processing.

Productivity measurements only indirectly or partially reflect economic growth stemming from products that did not exist before (as in the case of electronics and computers). Such measurements are especially misleading in electronics service industries, where the astonishing advances in price and performance are far more relevant than productivity. (Productivity is usually low in service industries anyway, because output is generally measured in terms of old definitions of factor output.)

The shape and structure of the arenas where so-called information industries compete is changing almost as we watch it. Rather than use such classifications as data processing and telecommunications, my colleagues and I have found it helpful to think of the industries as being made of various combinations of information providers and delivery system providers.

- *Information providers* are enterprises and organizations that develop and/or control data bases (including printed materials and electronically stored information) and libraries of audiovisual programs (including radio programs, records and tapes, films, videotapes, videodisks, and so on).

■ *Delivery system providers* are enterprises and organizations that develop and/or control pathways or "conduits" for information flows or that offer hardware and software systems for the delivery of information services.

■ *Information services* are those in which the perceived economic value to the user—that aggregation of determinants which meet the customer's wants and objectives and lead to a purchase decision—is based upon the delivery of information.

In the overall framework of international commerce, a user-friendly environment probably depends as much upon the regulatory climate and infrastructure as on other incentives.

Any enterprise that does business internationally needs the ability to move information in and out of the country quickly, at reasonable costs, and with the assurance that the rules of the game won't change drastically. International business might look at such factors as the stability of hospitable regulatory climate, low cost of compliance with necessary regulations, compatibility of information systems with local infrastructure, and infrastructure that includes superior international information and communications facilities. In addition to the incentives that are inherent in a reasonable regulatory climate with a favorable infrastructure, tax incentives tend to be the most attractive to business management because they allow the greatest flexibility.

By formulating overall national goals and objectives in the context of the technical and economic imperatives' driving growth in information use, a nation's policymakers can avoid costly cul de sacs, optimize potentials for domestic users, and maximize understanding of user requirements internationally. Senior management, labor leaders, and government officials share a pivotal role in formulating purposeful national goals and re-thinking measurement systems to fit the new realities. With many notable exceptions, senior management has been satisfied to let middle management worry about the nuances of information technology and its use. It is critical to capture the attention of business leaders—by raising the issues and by creating incentives—if any real progress is to be made.

Constructive input from labor on the use of the technology is also needed to develop new, more humanistic ways to increase production through microelectronics, to minimize the costs of the necessary social adjustments of adopting any new technology, and to improve the work experience.

Raising the User's Consciousness

Managers, manufacturers, laborers, civil servants, scientists, engineers, professionals, creative artists, students, and citizens will be the main beneficiaries of the new technologies, and they deserve the very best it has to offer.

For managers of domestic industry, the capabilities of information technology need to be made accessible. Middle and especially senior managers must be brought up to date about what can be done. While savings and increases in productivity can be considerable, so are the costs of adopting the new technology in an uncertain business climate and at a time of high interest rates.

For labor, which recognizes the need for the technology as well as its impact on the livelihood of so many people, special encouragement and safeguards might be considered. Often the new technology can mean that jobs are lost in one locale and gained in another. Retraining, relocation, and redundancy compensation are only palliative solutions, and locating major new plants to re-employ workers is seldom economically feasible. With the possibilities of advanced communications at hand, attention might be given, for example, to supporting the development of non-geography-dependent data bases and information services aimed at offering real economic value and at sparing severe disruption in the lives of workers.

For civil servants, the principal difficulty lies in the universal problem of bureaucratic inertia. Requiring that workers demonstrate information technology competence in order to be considered for promotions and providing in-grade salary incentives might be even more important than divisional commitment to employ technology.

For science, engineering, and technical professions, government might consider providing actual information hardware and such services as national data banks, as well as facilitating international links like the Oxford/CERN satellite transmissions.

For education, certainly one of the most tradition-bound sectors of society, the economies of electronic library facilities cannot be overlooked. And additional student aid for computer and information technology training on campuses should also be considered.

For "everyman" (and woman and child), the new technology offers numerous opportunities for a better and more interesting life. Production of consumer items from hand-held calculators to electronic games will be increasingly needed to meet market demand and for their educational value.

One way for government to raise public awareness of the capabilities for using and leveraging information technology would be to investigate the possibility of installing intelligent audiovisual, full-transaction-capable systems for the use of government agency staffs.

The U.S. House of Representatives, 75 percent of whose members already have terminals for accessing various internal government as well as external data bases, has considered installing a videotext capability for similar purposes. The opportunity for exerting leadership by beginning to identify and set very visible precedents around highly leveraged user needs is considerable.

THE SUPPLY SIDE

The very large-scale requirements and the need for long-term continuity in investment conditions in high-technology, high-value-added, and short-product-cycle industries indicate the need for world markets to provide an appropriate R&D base. In an increasingly competitive world, where nationalism is a powerful force, business risk and opportunity related to information technology are becoming more important globally than nationally.

The outlines of international strategies—both explicit and implicit—are beginning to emerge under three headings: national economic policies, national sovereignty concerns, and protection of individual privacy.

National Economic Policies

National economic policies focus on both the supplier's and the user's side, and are aimed at developing, nurturing, and protecting indigenous producers of information and communications hardware as a potentially major sector of the economy. They also are designed to ensure that information-intensive segments of the economy will be protected from enterprises with superior information and communications resources based outside the company.

On the information supplier's side, there is a marked contrast, for example, between the policies of the United States and Japan. Japan has clearly given its native industry broad-based support and incentives. The United States, far from seeking to consolidate and support its industries, sought for a dozen years to break up its information technology and communications giants, IBM and AT&T, through antitrust actions.

Elsewhere in the world, IBM and Japanese industry are seen as the major competitors to domestic hardware industries, with German, French, and the mid-size American firms operating on a more or less equal footing. It is generally felt that national companies need a substantial share of their own markets and considerable market penetration abroad to remain large enough to keep pace. Among less developed countries (LDCs) there is a trend toward developing modern information technology industries as a matter of national pride, along the lines of nuclear technology, "modern" armed forces, and such visible symbols as national airlines.

On the user's side, in economic sectors that depend heavily on data processing and communications (such as finance, insurance, and shipping), nations are also developing a protectionist stance. Governments fear that data processed abroad means lost domestic business. This sentiment is especially prevalent in Europe and Canada. The typical national responses have been to place unequal restrictions on the import and export of data while facilitating in-country processing.

National Sovereignty

National sovereignty issues are a second area around which a pattern of behavior is forming. Now that international satellite transmissions have been a reality for some time, the capacity to electronically transmit massive amounts of data is tending to blur international borders. Sovereign states are increasingly concerned about losing control over the information available to citizens. Nations also fear that their cultural integrity, their ability to maintain a national heritage when dominated by outside information forces, is threatened. The attempts by LDCs to restructure the Western world's media and the case of Canada trying to ignore U.S. media dominance are prime examples.

The fact that information technology is increasingly important to national security is raising another set of issues, including: What worst-case capacity must a nation have to ensure its independence? How can defense capability be enhanced through information systems, which are of prime importance for surveillance and verification of treaty agreements in arms control? Should information technology export be put under the same controls as nuclear and military technology?

Privacy of the Individual

Individual privacy issues have received considerable attention within some European countries and the United States, and plans are pending through OECD and the EEC. Coordination of individual national efforts will be imperative to a viable and orderly international system. The danger is that there may be a tendency to use the very legitimate privacy issue as a justification for non-tariff barriers and to provide national controls on the ingress and egress of data.

EFFECTS ON BUSINESS
AND INTERNATIONAL COMPETITION

Large corporate users who do business around the world have reacted to the policy conditions outlined above, and to the prospect for further restrictive initiatives, by seeking to minimize their risks in the face of actual and potential constraints in their ability to do business. On a country by country basis, policies may function (sometimes unintentionally) as non-tariff barriers to trade.

Whether a case involves Brazilian procurement preferences, or Japan's requirement that data be transmitted in a batch instead of an on-line mode, or French reporting requirements concerning data banks, the net result is a competitive edge for domestic industry. And the area of privacy protection may force corporations to reveal the information they have on each other, impose possible liability for unintended misuse of data (even by third parties), and put restrictions on data transmission across borders.

Similarly, national telecommunications policy can create serious impediments to the normal course of business. The telecommunications monopolies, which by and large generate their own revenues, have been responsible for some major blockages to the free flow of data. Plagued by the "fast-moving-technology/obsolescent-plant" syndrome, concerned about the explosive growth of private networks, and fearful that allowing extra-national data processing is tantamount to throwing away jobs, these public monopolies seem to tend toward a pattern of discriminatory tariffs with significant usage restrictions. Several potential consequences could result from such policies at the enterprise level, including:

- Border taxes to compensate for local job losses when data is processed outside the country of origin.
- Loss of flexibility in network reconfiguring and data processing planning.

- Generally negative influence on the growth of electronic mail and electronic funds transfer.

Probably owing in large measure to sensitivity to the trends toward privacy legislation and user restrictions imposed by national monopolies, data processing and communications planners so far have tended to develop strategies that give up the benefits of economies of scale and the synergies of full on-line networks and systems; they opt instead to distribute data processing operations by country, finding the most expedient means available where it has been necessary to move data across borders.

The central questions that need to be answered concerning artificial and uneconomic restrictions are:

- What are the real additional costs, lost profits, and lost opportunity to the enterprise?
- What are the costs and lost benefits to economies and society as a whole?

Although most corporate behavior is still in the anticipatory state, we have encountered several real-world stories that may be helpful in getting a sense of what is happening. Some of the following examples are illustrative of the direction that privacy protection practices can take:

- In Sweden, a catalogue containing the name, title, address, and tax assessment on all citizens with an income over a certain amount (tax information is public in Sweden) has been published annually for several years. The catalogue was to be sent in tape form to be printed by a firm in the United Kingdom, because no Swedish firm could cope with the desired deadlines. The Swedish Data Inspection Authority denied export.

- A German multi-national firm established in a subsidiary in Sweden a central personnel information system for administration and planning; it contained, for payroll purposes, normal information on employees' nationality, family, skills, and so forth. The Swedish Data Inspection Authority denied export.

- One of my firm's clients, a financial enterprise, is factoring into its strategic plan an extreme-case scenario of constrained international data flows.

- A consumer products company, generally self-contained within each country in which it operates, was able to negotiate agreements to support operations in three EEC countries remotely from a central location in Germany, because German standards are equal to or better than standards in those three countries.

- A diversified electronics and communications company has had no major problems as yet, but is incurring significant additional costs for recordkeeping, administration, backup systems, and security. It closely monitors specific new and impending initiatives such as the one in Austria, which proposed to regard the corporation as a "person." It systematically reviews the general worldwide situation to minimize risk to present operations and to keep apprised of the status of information services business opportunities.

- Another electronics company has also been incurring

significant costs for recordkeeping and the like in Europe and Taiwan, and it too is systematically reviewing information services business opportunities. In addition, the company has been frustrated by nontariff barriers, such as the Brazilian requirement for using only Brazilian terminals in communications networks.

- A medical products company that has effectively decentralized its worldwide processing operations has found that most records and summaries are not required on an immediate on-line basis via electronic media, and that mailing paper-based records protects secrecy while obeying the letter of the law.
- A diversified consumer products company rented a house that straddled the border of two European countries to maintain the option of having computer tapes in the venue most expedient to management purposes.
- A high official of a worldwide bank found it expedient to smuggle computer tapes out of an African country, and never did learn for certain if the resistance to moving those tapes across the border was general government policy or if it originated in Customs in that nation.

From the preceding discussion, it should be clear that there are two conflicting trends in the development of information technology. New opportunities for users are abundant in both domestic and international applications, but the policies of several nations are putting severe restrictions on use. This conflict points to what may be a major opportunity for countries to enhance their economic viability by developing policies that avoid nationalistic traps and actively promote the use of information technology.

FACTORS FOR SUCCESS
IN HIGH-TECHNOLOGY INDUSTRIES

The cost/benefit realities of major investments in any technology are not always obvious. Some investment conditions are relatively impervious to infusions of large amounts of cash. There may be a lesson to be learned from the fact that at the time the United Kingdom was investing in the Concorde, it could have bought 50 percent of all 20 of the largest U.S. aerospace companies with the same amount of money, as reflected in the market price of those securities.

No one who has approached the semiconductor business in an effort to prevail by force of large capital has succeeded. General Electric, Sylvania, ITT, Raytheon, and Philco Ford each invested $50 million to $100 million to develop semiconductors, with little success. In contrast, the largest equity market financing for National Semiconductor Corporation, a success story, was $10 million, and the company had been started with much less.

It might be interesting and useful for policy planners to prepare case studies of expenditures and results of other efforts in France, Japan, Germany, the United Kingdom, and the United States, and conduct comparative analyses of the conditions that either hinder or promote innovation, technical dynamism, and commercial success in new high-technology efforts. The ultimate goal must be to benefit the social and economic fabric of the nation by promoting accessibility to the very best information resources and technology for industry and citizenry.

Chapter 4

SEVENTEEN POSSIBLE FUTURE STATES

What will our future world be like? How will technology influence our social patterns, our government, our economic climate, the workplace, the quality of life? Computers are already changing our perceptions of time and space, and they are certain to shape our view of the world in even more fundamental ways. Looking ahead provides a fertile context for exploring the role of technology in our lives today. From an enormous range of future possibilities, seventeen are highlighted here.

This talk was presented to a meeting of clients of The Diebold Group, Inc., in New York City on October 16, 1979.

We stand on the threshold of becoming a "wired nation." Information technology already plays an important part in how we do business, how we work, and how we play. Whole new industries have burgeoned because of the computer and have brought new, previously unthought-of careers and occupations with them.

As computers become more and more capable of communicating with each other, distance and geography become less significant; "remoteness" takes on a whole new meaning. As intelligent terminals become smaller, cheaper, and more efficient, the physical location of a worker becomes almost inconsequential. Instant shopping, instant credit, and a cashless society—all on the way to being achieved—vastly change the economic traditions of consumer and merchant alike.

The following 17 possible future states have been chosen from a large number of possibilities. They are intended to stimulate thought and provoke speculation on what an information oriented world might be like, during our lifetimes and beyond.

1. The Entrepreneurial Work Force

Information technology opens the door for the individual "knowledge" worker to be highly selective about the work he or she performs. Many such workers will follow their entrepreneurial instincts, perhaps by becoming consultants or contractors and working for their previous employers. This will give the individuals the flexibility to perform their functions at their own convenience, in many instances off the premises of the employer. It is probable that such workers will receive a guaranteed annual wage in return for a commitment of a specified level of service to a prime employer, which may be a broker, an individual user, or an organization.

As individual entrepreneurs, knowledge workers will have far more independence than they would under other arrangements, which can help them avoid the "information obsolescence" that will become an increasingly difficult problem for employers and workers alike.

2. The Office Communications Center

Increasingly, each individual white-collar workstation will become a computer and communications center, complete with its own terminal and communications capabilities. Through this center, a worker can receive and send information and instructions and perform many job tasks. However, the nature of many of the tasks will itself change as a result of the new capabilities. For example, in a transcontinental meeting via television—"teleconferencing"—a team of executives could consider the wording of a report or letter, make the desired changes in text on a CRT terminal, and then immediately have the text typed (or printed) in their own offices or in the offices of the recipient.

Televised transcontinental meetings are already a reality. The Metropolitan Regional Council, an organization of regional government representatives, operates a facility at its headquarters (in New York's World Trade Center) through which members can interface with the main office or with each other via voice and video transmission.

Access to data bases will allow an executive to call up

historical data, industry statistics, and current operating information as needed, make modeling ("what-if?") analyses, and conveniently perform a variety of data manipulations without ever leaving the office. Furthermore, there is no technical reason (and little economic reason) why such capability could not be located within the executive's home, to supplement or even replace a traditional office.

3. Office Building Communications Facilities

The need for sophisticated and flexible communications capabilities in office buildings may lead to the emergence of real estate entrepreneurs as key retailers of computer and communications services. The real estate entrepreneur would purchase key communications services at wholesale rates based on volume purchasing power, and sell the services to building tenants.

For example, owners could include in their building:

- A large-scale computerized PBX for the entire building, complete with all advanced services.
- Connection to all major networks, such as those provided by AT&T, MCI, ITT, Satellite Business Systems (SBS), Tymnet, Telenet, and so on.
- Word processing centers connected to a variety of electronic mail services which are available to the entire building.
- A satellite disk on the roof.

This development will enable middle- and small-size businesses to access sophisticated services at cost levels similar to those for large organizations. The providing entrepreneur will earn revenues through rebates from major vendors and through markups added to the wholesale charges.

4. Worker Independence

Advances in information technology and communications will accelerate an existing trend toward greater worker independence. This will manifest itself in several ways: variable hours and work schedules, particularly in white-collar jobs; greater worker emphasis on leisure and educational activities on and off the job; worker pressure to opt for reduced or compacted hours, with appropriate salary adjustments; and increased pressure on employers to tailor remuneration (particularly benefits packages) to meet the needs of individual workers.

All of the changes will make the personnel administration function far more complex than it is today, but information technology will make it possible for the organization to meet many of the demands in a cost-effective manner. Organizations that do not provide such options may find themselves at a competitive disadvantage in the labor market.

5. Impact of Technology on Existing Industries

Information technology will significantly affect many existing industries both positively and negatively. It will do so in two major ways: first, by influencing the *ways* in which business is conducted (as it has already begun to do), and second, by affecting the *types* of business for which there is a demand.

Some examples: Every aspect of the publishing industry will undergo dramatic changes, primarily in the manner in which the final product is delivered. As only one example, the publication of service and repair manuals—which have an important impact on producers of capital goods—will change. Instead of voluminous manuals of thousands of pages, the document accompanying a piece of equipment could consist of just a few pages containing references to central data bases where needed information can be electronically accessed from on-site workstations.

Publishing could become a selective, supply-on-demand industry. This will have broad implications for newspapers, magazines and periodicals, books, advertisers, the paper and print industries, and other industries that are directly or indirectly involved in and peripheral to publishing.

The travel industry will be profoundly affected by a basic substitution of broad-band communication for business travel. This may impact negatively on airlines, car rental services, hotels, restaurants, and travel agencies. On the other hand, there will be important restructuring of priorities in the kinds and quantities of energy requirements and in the design and construction of office buildings and business centers.

The leisure industry will be affected by the ability of the consumer to stay at home and select, from any number of channels, virtually any form of the performing arts. This may negatively affect theaters, night clubs, and other centers where people gather for entertainment. On the other hand, the demand for entertainment in a wide variety of forms will be insatiable.

The retailing industry will also change dramatically.

Consumers will be less inclined to shop in person as the capability of electronically viewing merchandise at home increases. Mail order catalogues will be replaced by electronic catalogues.

There is every likelihood that banks as we know them today will not exist in 20 years. The information network capabilities that will be available in the future will enable corporations to perform their own banking services or utilize those provided by other corporations. Similarly, individuals could be in the business of providing financial services to other individuals through national networks.

6. The Business Office in the Future

As communications capabilities become more sophisticated and the human/machine interface becomes more natural, it will become less and less necessary for workers and executives to be physically located at work centers. Managers, as well as clerical workers, could spend several days a week at a remote work center near or in their homes, as opposed to commuting to offices in central business district.

The use of time- and geography-independent systems could lead to widespread decentralization of many office functions. People previously unable to travel to central cities (for example, homemakers and physically handicapped people) could become part of an office work force that works at home and electronically transfers the final product to wherever it is needed.

Such trends should have a serious impact on traditional aspects of work. Reduced physical contact could lessen corporate loyalty, for example. Worker morale would be affected (positively or negatively, depending on the circumstances) by removing the social aspects of office work.

Eventually the trend away from centralized work areas could lead to a redefinition of the roles, as well as the structures, of suburbs and central cities.

7. The Tailor-Made Newspaper

Readers will be able to tailor newspapers and magazines to suit their specific needs. Recent advances in information gathering and transfer, coupled with dramatic changes in printing technology, have led to many changes in the print media, including greater frequency of editions, custom-tailored local editions (community, state or regional), and simultaneous publication of regional editions transmitted by facsimile or other electronic processes.

Extending these trends—and given the technological base for further evolution—it would seem likely that newspapers and magazines would aim their sights at adjusting the content of publications to meet the needs and address the interests of specific readers or groups of readers (for example, an "oil" edition of *The Wall Street Journal,* or a "national politics" edition of *The Washington Post,* or a Chicago edition of *Time*). The flexibility offered by existing information processing techniques makes this technically if not economically feasible.

Beyond this, the next stage is to allow an individual reader to order a publication designed to meet his or her needs on a specific day, through a transmission and reproduction system that allows a newspaper drawn from an existing "menu" of news and feature items to be printed in the home or office.

8. Deterioration of Workers' Knowledge

Information technology will play a major role in addressing a problem for which it is partly responsible—the rapidly deteriorating value of a worker's knowledge due to new discoveries and other advances in any particular field of expertise. This will be an ever more acute problem among information workers; without extensively updating their knowledge, workers' years of highest value to employers will be those immediately following a period of formal education—exactly when they have the least experience.

As workers themselves become aware of the declining value of their knowledge, they can be expected to place greater demands on their employers for company-paid educational programs to help them avoid technological obsolescence. Indeed, the availability and quality of such programs will likely become a recruiting tool, one with more potential than many traditional fringe benefits.

In disciplines where the danger of technological obsolescence is particularly acute, workers may come to demand a change in traditional remuneration patterns to draw higher compensation in the earliest years of their employment, when their knowledge is most current and hence most valuable to the employer— much in the way that a professional athlete's salary declines as he passes his physical prime.

Experiments with employer-supplied worker education are already being conducted. The University of Southern

California conducts two-way video classrooms, with communication set up between the University campus and the satellite classrooms located on the company's premises.

9. Business Communication and Training in the Home

Closed-circuit television and video recording and playback capability will enable a business to shift some of the educational functions now conducted on the premises to the homes of its employees. Such offerings will undoubtedly extend beyond formal in-house training programs; they could include, for example, seminars in marketing, business law, economics, and similar topics for professional employees.

As economics and available channels permit, the initial offerings could be specific courses scheduled at specific times of the day (which, with timed recording capability, might be 3:00 A.M. for subsequent playback), or through tapes delivered directly to the employee for playback at his or her convenience.

"Addressable" video messages are not yet feasible on a commercial scale, but when they are, a business could use the video system to deliver a specific message, live or recorded, to a single employee, groups of employees, or the entire work force, in their homes. This capability will result in a radical restructuring of the traditional employee communications function.

10. Correspondence Schools Using Interactive TV

Large-scale two-way television, in combination with existing video recording and playback capability, will lead to a resurgence of correspondence schools on a level never before realized. They will become a practical alternative for many students for whom the cost of a traditional college education has become prohibitive.

Some universities are already providing college-level instruction in remote communities via video presentation, but far more sophisticated techniques will soon become technically and economically feasible. It will become possible for a student to achieve the full equivalent of a college education—including selective post-graduate work—in his home, with perhaps only a brief period spent on a campus for testing, special instruction, and so on. More and more students will take advantage of this option.

Particularly important to the success of such a system will be its ability to update the individual student's education on a periodic basis, to prevent technological obsolescence.

11. Home Purchasing of Products and Services

Consumers will use their own computerized home communications centers to evaluate, select, purchase, and receive a wide variety of goods and services. Energy costs, traffic, and crime will make it increasingly desirable to shop at home for products and services, while computer and communications technology will make it increasingly feasible to do so.

Interactive TV allows the seller to present an item to the consumer directly, and allows the buyer to place an order electronically. Commercial television will offer far more opportunities for direct purchase than it presently does. This trend will accelerate as it becomes easier for the potential customer to place an order directly through the TV cable or through the home computer.

In addition to conventional commercial messages, selective catalogue shopping by television will become feasible through pre-recorded videotape and cable TV channels devoted to the display of merchandise. The popularity of this capability will grow as it becomes feasible for the buyer to isolate the product in which he or she is most interested without having to go through many items which are of no interest.

Shopping in person will continue for big-ticket items and for those where personal taste is an important consideration, although the increasing cost of sales labor (which is difficult or impossible to automate) will place a huge premium on such services.

Improvements in the size, sensitivity, and costs of terminals, and in the transmitting power of communication satellites, will permit, at reasonable costs, the widespread direct reception of all kinds of information, including television programming.

The implications of these technical developments will be profound for both the business and residential marketplace. In effect, a virtually unlimited number of channels will be directly accessible from the television receiver. That holds enormous possibilities for all information media, for education and training, and for business.

Marketing of consumer products will undergo significant change because of several key characteristics of at-home purchasing:

- Much of the "economic privacy" of individual buyers and corporate suppliers will be eliminated, resulting in more volatile markets and a shift of power to the consumer at the expense of the supplier.

- Electronic market access, divorced from traditional distribution costs, will encourage the acceleration of small (fewer than five people) professional service organizations.
- There will be major changes in retailers' product mixes and distribution mechanisms: Generic products will be delivered from central distribution points, which will be used by several retailers that duplicate each other's sales of these products; general delivery service will return.

12. The Library Network

In the future, the library will become both more and less important as a repository of human knowledge. The library of the future will have its roots not so much in today's collections of books as in the existing commercial and academic information access systems, such as *The New York Times Information Bank* and similar services. The most significant aspect of such library networks will not be the fact they they will include a broad variety of media, ranging from printed matter to videotape and audio recordings. Rather, it will be that users will be able to access information by telephone or computer terminal for direct display in their homes and offices.

As the cost of personal services rises, both public and private libraries will undoubtedly be forced to cut costs; all but a handful will probably turn over their research and archival functions to computer-based information access services that connect the resources of more than one library into vast data bases that no single institution could easily afford. Tomorrow's libraries will tend to resemble museums more than research centers.

13. The Emergence of National Universities

Rapidly climbing costs will make it increasingly attractive for universities to form close working relationships with schools in other geographic areas. The strength and depth of such linkages will be directly related to the efficiency of communications channels among the institutions. Existing cooperative computer networks are in this context a tentative first step in the direction of national universities with geographically dispersed campuses.

The networks will be created to hold down costs by sharing resources and will enable the institutions to compete more effectively for the educational dollar—not only with other schools but also with the educational programs of the business sector. Through closed-circuit television, for example, a school might offer the services of a nationally renowned academician that no individual university could afford.

Similarly, communications and information processing capabilities might permit national or regional schools to achieve other economies of scale not otherwise possible.

14. Instant Product Testing

For many kinds of computer goods, point-of-purchase (POP) terminals will enable manufacturers to reduce product test time drastically. Such terminals will provide meaningful sales data virtually immediately after a product's introduction in a given market, while constantly monitoring sales performance. Instant product testing will tend to reduce product development lead times, but it will also tend to decrease the shelf-life of many products as new products are developed, tested, and brought to market.

Point-of-purchase data gathered through product codes will also allow manufacturers to evaluate the market desirability of alternative product features and pricing strategies, bringing a degree of precision to the marketing function that previously was not feasible. Such knowledge could also permit marketing and advertising merchandising approaches to be more specifically tailored to the needs and desires of specific markets than has been practicable before.

Marketing research studies will also be conducted by means of interactive television.

15. Personal Use: Computers in the Home

Although it will be some time before the personal computer is as ubiquitous as the telephone, computers are appearing in more and more homes in the form of stand-alone units, terminals, or interactive TV links (videotex). In addition to assuming many common household record-keeping activities, such as bank account reconciliation and maintenance of tax records, the home computer may also take over the control and monitoring of a variety of household activities, particularly in the areas of services, supplies, and security. For example, the home computer will eventually be used to track inventories of needed supplies, such as fuel oil, and automatically order new supplies. It could provide such services as automatically timing the preparation of meals, turning lawn sprinklers on and off, controlling temperature and humidity, monitoring energy consumption, and so on.

Burglar- and fire-alarm systems can also be linked to the computer to give automatic contact with the appropriate officials. In Woodlands, a suburb of Houston, such services are among a comprehensive TV package being offered to cable TV subscribers. And in Buffalo, New York, a meter-reading and energy-monitoring system is in place as a joint effort by the local cable TV company and the public utility.

16. Changes in Social Values

Information technology will lead to significant changes in social values in such areas as the work ethic, views on material possessions, and the desire for privacy. Since it will be possible for workers to structure jobs to meet their own convenience and preference, society will gradually move away from a "nine-to-five" orientation, a five-day work week, and a summer vacation. An individual's employment will become less important as a matter of personal identity or a measure of social worth. People will be known by their personal interests—skiing, guitar playing—rather than by what they do for a living. On the other hand, the ability to purchase those rare goods and services with a substantial human labor component will tend to become a new criterion for economic success.

Individual privacy and choice will become far more

important social considerations, with invasion of privacy likely to become not only a much more serious breach of social etiquette than is now the case, but, more importantly, an area of increased legislation.

17. Participative Democracy

Interactive television technology may lead to some radical changes in our system of representative democracy, to meet citizens' demand for a greater voice in decisions affecting them. On a test basis (in Columbus, Ohio), the mechanism already exists for individuals to express their opinions on specific issues through a cable television system.

If one were to extrapolate this trend, an elected representative could poll constituents for their views on specific controversial issues, thus reducing the role that the politician's own judgment, personality, and political instincts would play in the political process. This could lead to formal referenda on significant issues at the local, state, or federal level. The results might not be binding on the government, but the voice of the people would certainly have a strong influence on the decisions that are made.

Chapter 5

INFORMATION TECHNOLOGY: UNLEASHING A NEW ERA OF COMPETITION

Although many companies are beginning to perceive computer technology as a competitive weapon, for the most part it is still managed within a relatively narrow technical framework. How do managers bridge the organizational gap between the data processing shop and the corporate boardroom? The task becomes ever more critical as computers revise the parameters of competition in more and more industries. The situation opens an unprecedented opportunity for the entrepreneurial information executive— not to do a first-class job at yesterday's business, but to anticipate how we will do business tomorrow.

This speech was delivered to the 64th plenary meeting of the Diebold Research Program in Kiawah, South Carolina, on October 19, 1984.

The blinding pace of technological change is creating new opportunities and wholly new industries almost overnight. At the same time, it is changing the way all kinds of businesses are building a new competitive edge. Information technology—an amalgam of computer and communications—is altering the competitive structure of *all* industries and services, and just as rapidly is changing as an industry itself. It is a tool that corporate and financial officers and MIS executives can use to their organizations' advantage, yielding new strategies, increased profitability, and new business prospects.

While many companies are beginning to recognize information technology as a competitive weapon, for the most part it is still managed only within a relatively narrow technical or organizational framework. There is still a very wide gap between the current applications and the potential opportunities that information technology represents. Closing that gap will become an economic imperative as information technology becomes one of the key determinants of competitiveness through the remainder of this century.

One of the reasons information technology is still managed within a limited technical context, and not in a strategic business context, is that senior management has an imperfect understanding of the technology's relationship to corporate performance. Management faces a threefold dilemma:

1. While top managers often proclaim in corporate reports that information technology helps their firms stay competitive, they concede that these observa-

tions are largely based on "gut feelings." They are unable to support those feelings with solid measures or statistics. Without such measures, their approach to the technology remains tentative.

2. On a larger plane, executives find it difficult to grasp the way information technology is revising entire industry sectors and changing the external environment in which they compete. It becomes hard to visualize the big picture.

3. Even if information technology is accepted as a strategic concern, the challenge is to steer it toward new business opportunities. Rather than remain wedded to yesterday's business practices, managers need to rethink products and processes with an eye to tomorrow's opportunities.

Where does the executive find individuals with the talent and experience to explore uncharted new opportunities? The first step is to examine what is happening in today's business environment, and the ways in which the technology is fundamentally revising business objectives, activities, and relationships—and therefore the bases of competition. I will start with three case examples drawn from my firm's consulting work, clients with whom I have some firsthand familiarity. Then I will explore six ways in which information technology has changed the competitive landscape, and some practical strategies for deploying the technology to further the mission of the enterprise, enhance its offerings, and improve its competitive posture. I will end with a set of questions that I think MIS directors ought to be posing to themselves and a set of questions that top management should be asking itself.

INFORMATION TECHNOLOGY AND THE COMPETITIVE ENVIRONMENT: THREE CASES

1. Prentice-Hall, Inc.

The first case is Prentice-Hall, a large U.S.-based, although international, publishing company. It is the largest producer of college textbooks in the world and it is a major business and professional book publisher. The Prentice-Hall case touches on virtually every aspect of the phenomenon of information technology as a competitive weapon. Let me give you a couple of examples.

One of the basic products of Prentice-Hall is a tax service, a loose-leaf text that is provided to law and accounting firms and to the tax and legal departments of corporations. It brings users up to date on changes in the tax laws, regulations, court cases, IRS rulings, and so forth. Prentice-Hall has one major competitor in this essentially bifurcated market: the other player in it is a clearinghouse service. Both firms' products are quite similar and are marketed in a very similar manner.

Very interesting changes are occurring in that market. The Prentice-Hall service has now been put on-line, so that it is being delivered in an on-line electronic mode as well as in the more traditional loose-leaf form. The new format was introduced with a very small investment: Less than $10 million was spent in going on-line and marketing this on-line service. Part of the reason for the low cost is that, for several years, the computer function at Prentice-Hall has been very alert and very good in what is an all-around well-managed company. It began years ago to handle all of its copy electronically.

The competitor never converted to electronic storage and handling of its product, so that its entry cost would be high at this point. Going on-line would require taking years of printed material and getting it all input into the data base, whereas the cost in Prentice-Hall's case was a couple of million dollars of reprogramming in order to change formats. For Prentice-Hall, what had initially been viewed as a cost-effective way of handling information internally became the foundation for making that data base commercially available. Less than 24 months elapsed from the time the decision was made to go on-line to when the service was implemented. Now, having an order backlog as heavy as it can handle, the firm's problem is one of adding capacity and not getting too far ahead in accepting orders until they can be safely handled.

Because the competitor hasn't begun to automate its tax service, Prentice-Hall may find itself enjoying an almost clean sweep of a market. The case will become all the more interesting as the competitor develops a retaliatory strategy. What had been a commodity business in a duopoly situation has been transformed via a considerable differentiation of product. The electronic technology has changed not only the net potential of the product, but all the financial and marketing aspects of it as well. I think the case is an excellent example of how information technology can radically change the terms of competition in a market.

Let me go a little further. Information technology can also be used to "lock in" the customer. Customers can order all kinds of Prentice-Hall reports and special products through electronic means. For example, if a tax case is decided this afternoon, the material shown on the video display screen by the end of the day describes the documents and material pertinent to the case that may be ordered. So the technology locks in the customer in two ways: by making it inconvenient or undesirable to switch to a competitor's less timely offerings and by providing the publisher with an opportunity to move additional products. Prentice-Hall has moved ahead in the market in a way that will prove to be all the more substantial in a couple of years, as it becomes increasingly costly for the competitor to apply catch-up strategies. At this stage it depends on Prentice-Hall's ability to continue to add adequate capacity, but it has nonetheless been a very effective way of changing the economics of a fairly traditional business.

There are other areas in which information technology is changing Prentice-Hall's way of conducting business: for example, in its use of teleconferencing to conduct business meetings. Typically, when a tax law is passed or a major change occurs in the tax system, Prentice-Hall holds a series of meetings all over the country, flying a team around to describe to customers at each location what the impacts are likely to be. Recently something different was tried: An excellent panel of experts in Washington, D.C., was linked via teleconferencing to meetings in a number of hotels across the country. The choice of the hotel chain where all the local meetings took place depended on which chain had the facilities to allow a large number of cities to participate in the teleconference simultaneously. Teleconferencing cut down on travel expenses and allowed for a more timely delivery of the information. Thus we see the technology's impact not only on publishing but on hotel competition. In other words, being equipped to handle teleconferencing becomes an important factor in getting local business meetings in hotel chains.

Information technology is also changing the way Prentice-Hall handles and delivers products. The company already offers floppy disks incorporated into books and is beginning to have books transmitted on disk. The changes required an analysis of the Prentice-Hall warehousing and distribution channels. As it happens, these are ideal for software, with the result that the company added large lines of software products for which it provides the warehousing, distribution, and, in some cases, the sales channels. It has added major throughput to a traditional, very tightly run distribution organization. It's an interesting case in that the technology has transformed a whole range of things, from the way the sales force operates on through changes in the product.

The changes also involve public policy issues that affect competition, including copyright law. In lobbying for modifications in copyright law, the company has tried to be consistent with its forecast of where the technology will be in a few years. Getting the law written in a way that allows a publisher some effective means of collecting copyright income, especially on advanced modes of distribution, is very important.

2. General Motors

While the impact of information technology is well documented in the information-intensive industries, such as banking and publishing, its impact on manufacturing and other industries is not as widely understood. Just look at the case of General Motors. Its $2.55 billion purchase of Electronic Data Systems Corp. (EDS), which was initially intended as a way of becoming a low-cost producer, was the first in a series of other investments made in companies in the information technology field, all aimed at improving GM's competitive posture.

At General Motors, three different trends are emerging, and they're very interesting from the standpoint of information technology.

- First, GM is relying heavily on information technology to hold down costs. EDS will help the auto maker integrate its manufacturing systems so that they speak a common machine language, while GM's investment in robotics and factory automation will further improve its cost performance.

- Second, technology is being embedded into the product in the form of on-board computers, resulting not only in product differentiation but also in major changes in the way automobile service will be handled in the future. The entire service structure, down through retailing, is going to be affected by this technology. The on-board computers will be able to diagnose problems, alert the driver to the need for service, and handle the invoicing, credit, and payment arrangement, all by electronic means.

- Third, GM is enhancing its ability, through the use of these systems in manufacturing, to tailor the order precisely to the customer's specifications. That has always been the theory, sometimes the practice, in the past, but it has become cumbersome and costly.

The ability now to manufacture unique custom vehicles in a cost-effective way is a new development.

Interestingly, General Motors plans a 10 percent reduction in health care costs through computerizing the Blue Cross/Blue Shield effort over the next three years—a 10 percent reduction in an area that has seen cost increases sometimes approaching 20 percent annually.

The computer capabilities that are beginning to be installed in automobiles afford a competitive edge to the manufacturers and dealers. The very wide array of possibilities includes not only various computer-generated messages that are spoken to the driver, but German-made "trip computers" that determine the routes for the driver to take. A larger percentage of the value of the automobile—perhaps 16 to 20 percent—will be determined by the onboard computer system.

3. American Hospital Supply

American Hospital Supply is a distributor for a wide range of products to hospitals. By installing its own terminals in the hospitals, and by doing so before its competition, the company was able to lock in the customer. Not only did the terminals make it easy for the customer to order supplies, but they made it possible to enhance that service by providing a series of software additions. American Hospital Supply dealt a major blow to Johnson and Johnson, which was put in the position of having to devise a retaliatory strategy. This is, I think, a clear example of the competitive value of information technology—as opposed to its value as a support function.

Competitive structure is changing in virtually all industries as a result of information technology. The changes have been most apparent in financial services and are becoming more apparent in publishing. However, as I hope these examples have illustrated, it's happening in other kinds of industries as well—not only in consumer industries but in capital group industries too.

The difference between companies that are leading and those that are lagging in deploying information technology relates to the way the issue is handled organizationally. MIS has the responsibility of looking at how to get management—particularly senior management and user management—to understand what's possible, what could be done. Meanwhile, CEOs are the ones who have been coming to my firm saying, "I know information technology is going to change my industry and my whole business. We are terribly well equipped with computer resources, and we do a very good job at the support function with MIS. But what I need is some kind of entrepreneurial function here to change what it is we are selling. Where do I look and how do I organize my approach to get there? We brought in very good talent on the traditional MIS side, but it's now a different game. Where do we go from here?"

SIX CHANGES IN THE COMPETITIVE LANDSCAPE

1. Incorporation of Information Technology into Products and Services

Computer functions are beginning to be embedded in all sorts of products. This is true not only for capital goods,

such as machine tools, but also for consumer durables—
and for some consumer nondurables as well. For example,
think of all of the home appliances in which microprocessors today function as timers. Tomorrow they are going to
play an absolutely vital role in the service operation,
because when the oven breaks it's going to place its own
phone call to the service company and it's going to go
through its own diagnostic routine with the service company's computer. And somebody may knock on the door
and say, "Pardon me, but your oven ordered a new heating
coil and here it is."

Of course, much of this is still on the drawing boards. In
part, the new capabilities are marketing devices and sales
devices, but they will change the service function. When a
shop-floor manager has trouble with the factory machinery
and it is possible to connect it to the supplier's computer
and to run through a set of diagnostics, that creates a whole
new ball game in the service function for capital equipment, quite apart from the consumer's service function. So
the technology affects not only performance features but
also service and credit arrangements.

Chips are being used in all manner of products, from
experimental ski boots that release the bindings automatically at certain G forces, to GE light bulbs that monitor
energy consumption. Visitors at Epcot will find Bell Labs
guideposts with touch-sensitive display screens offering
tourist information in a choice of languages. Just by touching portions of the screen, a visitor can obtain all sorts of
information and can gain access to a human being who
speaks that person's native language. In the Denver
Hilton, touch-screen computers in the lobbies are used in
the same way.

The computer's ability to respond to touch and voice keeps getting better and better. We need to learn more about linguistics, but in the 1990s we will have a wide array of devices that will be very easy for people to use by speaking, by touching, or perhaps at some point by thinking.

Vannevar Bush said that before the end of the century we would all have computer implants to connect directly to these systems. MIT has done a good deal of work on implanting computers in amputees. Today an amputee can simply think about moving his or her arm, and the artificial arm moves because of a linkage from the nerve system to the control system. If that's happening already, we will no doubt see a much, much wider range of options for activating and interacting with these systems.

2. Creation of New Products and New Services

In the course of studying industrial archaeology, I recently came across my 20-inch slide rule. I was holding an industrial artifact in my hands! Can you imagine being a slide rule manufacturer today? The field of information technology is, of course, filled with examples of new industries being created as a result of the technology. In the entertainment industry, the emergence of video games made for an industry that, even in its slump, was several times the size of the movie industry. Those involved in brand new industries must be receptive to the creation of new kinds of products and new kinds of services, which are frequently ignored by the principal players. Darryl Zanuck in 1946 summed up the entire movie industry's view of TV when he said, "TV won't be able to hold any market it captures after the first six months. People will soon get tired of staring at a plywood box every night." Of course, the movie industry has ended up being quite dependent upon the newer TV industry.

In the creation of new products and services, management must think in terms of software as well as hardware. Should a company like S. C. Johnson, for example, which deals very extensively with various kinds of household products, be thinking in terms of household robots? Are we going to have better systems for machine vision and better applications of artificial intelligence in this area? Should company management be thinking of that as a real product line? Probably. One must constantly focus on the customers' needs, not just current needs but those of decades from now, and of how the technology will change.

3. Altering Business Interrelationships

Take the case of banks that have used information technology to handle a large number of small depositors in a cost-effective way, and in so doing have transformed a previously unprofitable market into a lucrative new market and opened a new supply relationship. Citibank is a very good example of a supply relationship that was changed through creative use of new technology. A Citibank official told *The New York Times* on April 21, 1983, that Citibank "no longer considers itself a bank," but instead views itself as a provider of electronic services. In sports, Qantel's programs are being used by several of the major sports teams for supply analysis. Teams can conduct a very detailed analysis of the kind of players they want to acquire, using a sophisticated software package that analyzes team needs and matches them against each player's history. Publishers, too, are seeing similar changes in business relationships as they begin to accept and transmit manuscripts in the form of computer disks.

In terms of marketing and distribution channels, salespeople are able to ask questions by use of portable computer equipment directly from their homes or from the office of the prospect, and get immediate answers. For example, an insurance salesperson can use a computer to form-fit insurance policies to the prospect's needs on Saturday night, when the sale is hot, and make the sale in the prospect's home rather than waiting. Such cases are becoming typical.

Less attention has been given to cases of decision support use for marketing. For example, the Fingerhut subsidiary of American Can has about four times the return of any other direct mail company because of a very sophisticated software package that it has devised. The package allows the company to precisely match what it offers with the needs of individual customers. As a result, Fingerhut is achieving a net profit that is four times that of any of the competitive players in that game.

The airline reservation system called Sabre is a good example of vendor lock-in (mentioned earlier in this chapter). This system was developed by American Airlines and used by many independent travel agents. Because the Sabre system listed all American flights first, travel agents tended to book American flights for their clients. In the recent antitrust case, American was found to have an unfair competitive advantage because of this. The company was indeed achieving a substantial increase in sales because of the system, and realized that it was a marketing weapon. The trade press and industry observers viewed Sabre in the beginning simply as a way of handling the clerical work of reservations. Very few people realized that it was going to be a marketing weapon, but it was designed very well and was used very aggressively in marketing terms.

The identification of lucrative markets through better decision support systems is another aspect of the changing relationships among business units. A case in point is an insurance company that now uses computers to build an extensive data-base system to determine which potential markets will be profitable; the company had not previously differentiated by profit different classes of customers. Electronic shopping is another example of a changing relationship between supplier and consumer.

As society becomes more computer conscious, with many more computer-literate people than we had just four or five years ago, a company can also compete by identifying its products with the "Computer Age." The result is consumer products like breakfast cereals with the Pac-Man® or Donkey Kong® symbol on the box. Moreover, people are getting used to using computers in the travel industry, the hotel industry, and all of retailing.

Competitive relationships are changed by public policy issues, as discussed in detail in Chapter 2. Technology is outpacing regulation. Lobbying efforts and external affairs efforts should be focused on where the technology will be in a few years and what's going to be important to business people. Getting the legal structure and the regulatory structure modified in a way that is advantageous will be a very important part of using computer technology creatively in a competitive mode.

Copyright issues, privacy legislation, banking legislation, and a series of other public policy issues are very big determinants of profitability, and they're very big determinants of how aggressively computer technology can be used as a competitive weapon. For example, a judge ruled recently in upstate New York that a store chain's cash machines were bank branches, and the stores were forbidden to use the machines because of branching restrictions. The machines were linked to the bank so credit payments could be made in the stores, and it was an important part of the chain's strategy. The drug industry also illustrates how being able to respond more rapidly to FDA acceptance procedures is a very important competitive factor.

4. Defining One's Business

It sounds simple, but defining the mission or purpose of a business is probably the most difficult task company management faces. Consider this example in the history of the computer industry. In the late 1940s, a scientist named Fred Seitz, one of our great physicists who later became head of Rockefeller University, approached Ed Gee at DuPont. Ed Gee, who is now chairman of International Paper, was then running research for a division of DuPont. Seitz requested that DuPont grow pure silicon crystals, which were needed for advanced radar work. DuPont built a factory on 3,300 acres of land in a remote area of the South and commenced silicon production. It was the only source in the world, at that point, of pure silicon crystals,

some of which found their way into the hands of research-
ers at Bell Labs.

At that point, Ed Gee went to the management committee at DuPont, and said, "Look, we're the only source in
the world for silicon, and it's creating a completely new
industry. Let's move further on this." The management
committee of DuPont, in its infinite wisdom, said, "We've
defined the business of DuPont very carefully, and our
business is chemistry. Silicon crystals are in the realm of
physics. Sell it." And DuPont got out of the business. Five
years later, DuPont spent a large amount of money trying
to get back into the chip business. By then it was too late.

A company's definition of its business is absolutely crucial, and is being totally changed by our technology. This
the very heart of the question of how to use information
technology competitively. Jimmy Robinson, the chairman
of American Express, once said to me, "All the financial
analysts keep saying that we're in the financial services
business. They're wrong. American Express is in the information business. We're in the data processing business.
And if you think about the future, you've got to think about
it in those terms." Al Casey, the chairman at American
Airlines, echoed that sentiment: "We're supposed to be in
the transportation business. We're in the information business. Our most important competitive factor is the way in
which we handle the information to fill our seats. But we're
in the information business."

Very few people—but some very interesting people—
realize that information technology is a determinant of
what their business is. Let me bring up one final historical
example. In 1876, Alexander Graham Bell wanted to sell

the patents to the telephone. He thought about it for a long time, and he figured that the one place where people would understand what the telephone was going to do to society was Western Union. Western Union had been formed to transmit messages electrically, to transmit pulses in the form of telegrams. He approached Western Union and offered all the telephone patents at the low price of $100,000—and was turned down. Western Union said, "Who would ever want to talk by voice? The way we have these pulses going now is just fine. Who's going to use voice?" Bell then decided to start the telephone company. Western Union was a company that had been created not many years before, specifically around almost the same technology as Bell's inventions, but its managers couldn't visualize the market and couldn't see how the technology would change its business. Given that, one shouldn't be surprised by the difficulty of getting across the great impact of computers as a competitive weapon.

Take the case of Time, Inc. By redefining its business several years ago, when cable was coming in, Time ended up making a series of moves that, within a decade, became more important financially than all of its print offerings put together. Electronic media became much more important than all the great magazines of that empire, simply because Time redefined its business and how it was going to focus on information dissemination. At the moment, Time's effort is just one of the 300 experiments in the United States on teletext and videotex services. All sorts of firms are experimenting, and consolidations and new combinations of people are forming. This is obviously a time of tremendous turmoil, but clearly the outcome is going to be a major change in the way that products and goods are marketed. It's going to depend upon very good entrepreneurial talent.

5. Being a Low-Cost Producer

Obviously, we're all interested in doing things at the lowest cost, but traditionally there have been three approaches to devising effective competitive strategies: by establishing market niches, offering unique products, or being the low-cost producer. Traditionally, successful companies are the ones that identify exactly which of these strategies they're going to follow. Those that decide to be low-cost producers have all sorts of very interesting options available in terms of new information technology.

A little-known case example of using software to cut costs is an elaborate software package that Bell Labs devised for the telephone directory. AT&T has acted as a local supplier of directory service to the government and has booked very large-scale contracts in this area. Using the software package, which had initially been designed for internal use for the telephone books, made a dramatic change in cost. AT&T became the low-cost producer of the directory as a result, and the software aspect was crucial.

6. Information Resource Management

Information resource management (IRM) is one aspect of competitive strategy that has been virtually overlooked in the trade literature, even though the Diebold Research Program has been emphasizing its importance for close to a decade now. IRM involves viewing information as a management resource not unlike capital and labor, and it is probably one of the most important uses of technology as a competitive weapon. This concept is finally beginning to take hold in the United States, but Japan was much quicker to adopt it. Although I've always been a big skeptic of trying to copy Japanese technique, I think we can learn from their approach to IRM. The Japanese are extremely good at collecting information of all kinds and getting it to the right people in their organizations. They're adept at taking a variety of information from all over the world and channeling it back through the trading companies to the right places. That ability is at the heart of IRM.

FINAL QUESTIONS

There are two categories of questions we should consider: those senior managers ought to be asking and those MIS managers ought to be asking.

Senior Management

There are three categories of questions for senior management.

1. Questions about organization and staffing.

- Is there adequate information technology know-how in my business and my product planning functions to harness new opportunities?

- How can I best use the important information technology know-how that is in my MIS organization for the new strategic areas?
- What new attitudes and outlooks are needed in my MIS business and product planning organization and how can these best be developed?

2. *Questions about business strategies.*

- How and to what extent should my company's defined strategic objectives and market definitions be changed to encompass information technology potential and to preempt competitive encroachment?
- What new market and entrepreneurial opportunities exist in areas related to my business in which strategic use of information technology can be a significant advantage, and how should I pursue these?
- Where is my competition vulnerable from failure to capitalize on information technology potential, and what are the best strategic ways of taking advantage of their competitive lethargy?

3. *Questions about investment.*

- Are current investment guidelines, return on investment, hurdle rates, etc., likely to stifle or to encourage the correct information technology decisions in the strategic competitive area?
- Do competitive internal priorities for resource allocation of people, dollars and capacity squeeze out strategic applications?

MIS Management

What should MIS managers be asking? Their questions should address two major areas.

1. Organization and staffing.

- Does my current staff contain people with the know-how and the outlook necessary for a contribution in strategic areas, and do these people have proper visibility and incentives?
- How can we best support end-user computing to ensure a coordinated approach to corporate strategic opportunities?

2. Priorities and resource allocation.

- How can I develop properly focused strategic suggestions for top management with adequate credibility?
- And how can I develop management consensus on the proper allocation of scarce resources, between strategic and operational needs?

Action Steps

What kind of action steps can one take? There are three things that can be done. First, one can research how competitors are using information technology, through trade literature and other sources. Don't expect to be able to ask competitors directly, because not only will people be close-mouthed about it, but by and large they tend to misdirect and misinform their competition. Information technology becomes a highly proprietary, competitive area. My firm does consulting assignments on competitive issues for several companies, and the level of secrecy required on those projects approaches that of the work we do for manufacturing firms.

Second, one can review the existing portfolio of applications programs to see which, if any, could be used or modified to be employed as a competitive weapon. Some applications programs devised for one purpose can be highly useful as a competitive weapon.

Third, one can develop a program with end-user departments (which is, after all, where much of the entrepreneurial insight and outlook will occur), to begin to get users to realize what the possibilities are and to work with them in the development of business strategies.

During the 20-year life of the Diebold Research Program, the computer function has changed materially, not only from the standpoint of technology and costs, but also in the following ways:

- From a support function to a line-management responsibility.
- From a wholesale business to a retail business.
- From a technical to an entrepreneurial function.

And those three changes have occurred very suddenly, often with many of the same individuals playing key roles, but often without management thinking about it and looking at it in these terms.

Such changes affect what kind of people one wants to hire, what kind of development tracks to give them, what to do about bringing people from other parts of the organization through the data processing or MIS shops. It affects staffing and organizational issues materially, and I think one would be better off focusing on this in advance, rather than simply reacting to it as competitors do it, or as management begins to become more conscious of it. Simply put, we must look to the future.

One of the world's best-known futurists, my friend Arthur Clarke, devised something called Clarke's Law, which is that if an elderly and distinguished scientist says that something is possible, it almost always is, but if an elderly and distinguished scientist says something is impossible, he is very likely wrong. The history books are filled with comments such as Lord Kelvin's that radio has no future, and Edison's saying that the phonograph is of no commercial value and that the radio craze would die out in our time. When Edison invented the electric light, the gas companies saw their stock on the London stock exchange plummet, and Parliament appointed a committee to investigate electricity. The findings of the Parliament were that Edison's ideas were "good enough for our transatlantic friends, but unworthy of the attention of practical or scientific men." And in the immortal words of one of the Oxford Dons, Erasmus Wilson, "when the Paris Exposition of 1878 closes, electric light will close with it and no more will be heard of it." So beware of being too skeptical.

This spring I found a cartoon from *The New Yorker* in which one butterfly is saying to another, "You may be a butterfly, but you still think like a caterpillar." My final message is this: Don't be a caterpillar. Keep your eye to the future.

INDEX

139